THE SYMMETRY OF GOD

THE SYMMETRY OF GOD

Rodney Bomford

FREE ASSOCIATION BOOKS / LONDON / NEW YORK

First published in Great Britain in 1999 by
FREE ASSOCIATION BOOKS
57 Warren Street, London W1P 5PA

© 1999 Rodney Bomford

The right of Rodney Bomford to be identified as the author of this
work has been asserted by him in accordance with the Copyright,
Designs and Patents Act 1988.

A CIP catalogue record for this book is available from the British
Library

ISBN 1 85343 438 8 pbk; 1 85343 437 X hbk

Designed and produced for the publisher by
Chase Production Services, Chadlington, OX7 3LN
Printed in England by T.J. International, Padstow

To Gerald and Bruin Wooster
in gratitude for their wise friendship
over many years

The picture on the cover of the paperback edition is a fractal. Fractals are important in chaos theory through which order has been found within chaos. This book is based upon Matte Blanco's symmetric logic, through which order has been found within nonsense. What one does for physical science, the other does for logic. The defining feature of a fractal is the identity between a part and the whole, and that is central to symmetric logic too.

Spirals are also significant in the thinking of Carl Jung. In a mandala a clock-wise spiral expresses the unfolding of the unconscious into consciousness: that too is a theme of this book. Such may portray the revelation of the Eternal God among the things of time.

Contents

Acknowledgements

I acknowledge with pleasure a debt of gratitude to Ignacio Matte Blanco for the thinking which underlies this book, and for a brief friendship with him before his death. I am grateful, too, to the London Bi-logic Group which meets to study his work and carry forward his thoughts. The group was initiated by Eric Rayner and Gerald Wooster, who have both most kindly read this book in draft form, as have Daphne Turner, Charles Pickstone and Janet Unwin. To all five I owe thanks and also to the people of my church, St Giles Camberwell, who have enabled me to sit more lightly than I would like to parish duties during the past months.

We acknowledge, with grateful thanks, permission from the following to reproduce short extracts: Gerald Duckworth & Co. Ltd for *The Unconscious as Infinite Sets* by Ignacio Matte Blanco; Faber & Faber Ltd and Harcourt Brace for 'Burnt Norton' from *Four Quartets* in *Collected Poems 1909–1962* by T.S. Eliot; HarperCollins for *The Inner Eye of Love* by William Johnston; Oxford University Press for *Metaphor and Religious Language* by Janet Soskice; Routledge for *The Archetypes and the Collective Unconscious* and *Answer to Job* by Carl Jung; SCM Press for *Systematic Theology Vol. 1* by Paul Tillich; The Society for Promoting Christian Knowledge for *The Edge of Glory* by David Adam; and Thames & Hudson Ltd for *The Uses of Enchantment* by Bruno Bettelheim. If we have inadvertently reproduced other material that is in copyright we will be happy to make acknowledgement in future printings of this book.

The author welcomes discussion by e-mail:
bomford@alphaplus.co.uk

Introduction

Does the Christian faith speak of realities or fictions? Is God real or merely a verbal symbol? Those who speak for the church speak with voices contradictory as perhaps never before. Movements springing from the New Right in America emphasise the literal reality of God, while at the other extreme exponents of the Sea of Faith movement deny God any reality at all. Meanwhile the world's hunger for the spiritual, for an understanding of life that is not merely technological, turns to ever more varied, and often bizarre, sources for its satisfaction.

This book is written for those who are dissatisfied with the debate in the church, who look for an understanding of Christian faith which is neither literalist nor reductionist; that is to say, which neither clings rigidly to the literal truth of every word of the Bible, nor on the other hand reduces the faith by rejecting most of what the past has believed to be central. This book is an attempt to sketch an understanding of traditional faith in terms credible today. It is an attempt to transcend the division between the literalist and the reductionist.

Few church leaders and few theologians would subscribe to either of the extreme positions I describe above. Yet there is a lack of coherent accounts of the faith which do justice both to tradition and to how we think and feel ourselves to be in today's world. The adherent of a sect steps out of that world into a mental ghetto and the mainstream churches of a conservative type are becoming more and more like such sects.

From the beginning the church has borrowed philosophies from the world as handmaids to faith, and has expressed its faith through them. This has not only been to communicate to those outside, but also so that faith may understand itself. It has enabled believers both to believe, and yet to belong to the same world as their contemporaries. Philosophers from Plato to Heidegger have been used for this purpose, by theologians from the patristic period to modern times, and there is an abiding need for such expositions of the faith.

This book is an attempt to meet that need, or rather to sketch out how such a need might be addressed.

The first problem is to find an appropriate philosophy. Thomas Aquinas used Aristotle and his followers today use him still. In the twentieth century, notably Bultmann, Tillich and Macquarrie used existentialism, but neither Aristotelian nor existentialist philosophy express human self-understanding very widely at the present time. Indeed there does not seem any philosophy which has a general and popular attraction and academic philosophers are generally hostile to the kind of metaphysical system which theology has used in the past.

I contend that the work of Freud and Jung and their successors has bequeathed to today's world a way of understanding humanity that is very widely shared. It has its critics, but in a pluralist society no one scheme will suit everybody. It has had an enormous influence not only on writers and creative artists of every kind, but on the man and woman in the street. The idea that our thinking and feeling are influenced and rooted in an unconscious aspect of ourselves is very generally believed. It is psychoanalytic thinking that I propose as a 'philosophical' handmaid for Christian theology.

This approach was pioneered by Victor White in *God and The Unconscious* in 1949. Its influence was wide, but its fruitfulness was inhibited by the pre-Vatican II framework of White's work and the predominant place White gave to Jung. The two sides did not come close enough together.

A significant moment in British religious history was the publication of *Honest to God* by John Robinson in 1963. He drew on much that was commonplace in academic theology, but it came as a shock to the churchgoer and, still more, to the non-churchgoer who thought he or she knew what the church's God was like. God was not to be found, said Robinson, up there or out there, but in the depth of human life. This dominant metaphor of depth however he did not much elucidate. In particular he did not take up the psychoanalytic understanding that the depth of humanity is the Unconscious.

While theoretical theology has, for the most part, ignored psychology, the counselling movement which has a Freudian origin has pervaded pastoral theology. At the same time Jungian thinking has immensely influenced the recent growth in certain kinds of spirituality. Moreover it is surely 'within themselves' that most Christians would claim to know God, who has been described as the 'soul of our souls', the spirit within our spirit. There is therefore a strong case for using the 'science of the soul' to explore, to explain, to expound the concept of God.

The search for God within the soul or heart or spirit is an aspect of most of the great faiths of humankind: it is the path of mysticism. While few Christians would describe themselves as mystics, yet the writings of the mystics strike a chord in many. Such works as *The*

Cloud of Unknowing are widely read and a growing number of people in Britain are pursuing an arguably similar search for God in Buddhist dress. Mysticism of many kinds appears to penetrate regions of the mind that the psychoanalyst describes as unconscious. Within the soul there is a place of eternal stillness, of cosmic unity, which can be described only symbolically and paradoxically. The Christian mystic finds God in this place, the psychoanalyst may describe it as the Unconscious. I shall propose that the concept of God and the concept of the Unconscious have much in common and share, to a significant degree, the same kind of reality.

There may appear to be an unbridgeable chasm between the glory glimpsed by the mystic and the dark cellar of the Freudian Unconscious. However, Freud was a doctor and his writing predominantly describes the workings of those sick at soul. There are the germs of other possibilities in his work. These were grasped by Jung and developed with Byzantine complexity. The differences between the two men were many, but I suggest that they arise above all from the divergent thrusts of their interest. While Freud remained primarily a healer of the sick mind, Jung wanted also to explore the depths of the mind, sick or whole. Freud predominantly wrote of that part of the unconscious mind that arises from the repression of conscious experience too painful to retain in consciousness. Jung wrote also, and more so, of a collective Unconscious which is not the deposit of buried pain. While not ignoring Jung, I shall be returning to Freud's fundamental description of the Unconscious and shall find there certain relatively simple, but profound, principles of very wide application. I shall apply them to the language of faith.

Freud described five chief characteristics of the Unconscious. It has been little noticed, still less attended to by theologians, that one of these was that of eternity, a characteristic, one might say, that is almost definitive of the Christian God. To many who practise a religion, the search for the eternal, for something infinitely valuable in life, is at the core of their belief. As an old prayer puts it: 'may we who are fatigued by the changes and chances of this fleeting world, repose upon thine eternal changelessness.'[1] Many others no longer look to the church or any other faith for glimpses of the eternal, yet retain a longing and a wistfulness for what faith might offer, for what it once provided.

I shall be examining the eternal and the other characteristics of the Unconscious in Chapters 2 to 4. There may seem, nevertheless, to be a chasm between Freud's Unconscious and the Christian's God. To bridge it I shall pursue the thinking of Ignacio Matte Blanco, an analyst who has been described as the discoverer of the Freudian *unrepressed* Unconscious. His work is attracting growing interest in psychoanalytic circles. In particular he claimed that the unconscious mind has a logic of its own, which he called 'symmetric logic'. This is quite unlike the logic of common sense. At first sight it appears to be wholly nonsensical, but, on reflection, its presence may readily be discerned in emotional thinking. It is the logic of feeling and of the imagination.

Towards the end of *A Midsummer Night's Dream*, Theseus, the king, reflects that:

> The lunatic, the lover and the poet
> Are of imagination all compact.

They 'apprehend more than cool reason ever comprehends'.

Matte Blanco's symmetric logic describes the 'reasoning' of the lunatic, the lover and the poet. I argue that much discourse about God shares the same 'reasoning'. If it is to express the infinite and the eternal, theology cannot do without paradox, symbolism and myth. I hope to show that these are the means by which may be expressed the symmetric logic of the unconscious mind.

At this point I must warn the reader that many find symmetric logic difficult to understand. I have used some simple mathematical and logical concepts to expound it. Some readers may need to pause and play around a little with these concepts in order to grasp what symmetric logic is. It is not as intimidating as it may appear to some at first and it vastly illuminates one's understanding of the emotional interchanges of ordinary life. The rest of the book will be incomprehensible unless the reader has some grasp of it.

Having described symmetric logic at some length, I then examine the language of faith, by means of it. This is an immense field and huge and complex questions have been dealt with in a most summary manner. That has been necessary for, while the basic thesis is a relatively simple one, at least an indication needed to be given of how it may be worked out in the whole range of Christian faith: to leave out such matters as the doctrines of the Trinity and Incarnation, the practice of prayer or belief in life after death, would have left matters vital to the faith of many without a place in the scheme. I have, therefore, not attempted to engage at length in dialogue with particular modern theologies, but have referred only to what will best illuminate my main argument.

My intention is to accept the truths that historical research and rational inquiry have established, while at the same time clearing a space in which the faith of the church may be proclaimed, without apology, in full traditional dress. Faith is not furthered by defending the indefensible, but nor does it flourish when its imaginative richness is pared away. I propose that the work of Freud offers a basis which may allow theology to avoid both these defects and to engage in the present times with the enduring thirst of humanity for the eternal.

Note: I would hope that my language is gender inclusive. In discussing the traditional God of Christianity, however, I have used the male pronoun. I do not intend by this to attribute maleness to God and hope it gives no offence. Clumsy circumlocution is obtrusive, and I have not yet come upon an alternative.

1   Transcendence and Eternity

There are few harder tasks for the Christian in today's world than to explain what the word 'God' means to one who does not understand it. Since faith is seldom to be held without at least some shadow of doubt, some such dialogue must be conducted within the mind of the believer as well. Certainly there is vigorous debate within the churches about what God is: and the explanations propounded through Christian history by theologians and apologists for faith are infinitely various.

There are those who claim that God is a real being, invisible to the human eye, yet greater than any other, the source of the existence of all that is. His existence, they would admit, cannot be proved: for if it were proved faith would not be faith, but certainty, and faith must in the end remain as faith. Yet many have attempted, by rational argument, to claim that belief in God's existence is a reasonable explanation of the world, more reasonable than any other. Such an approach is particularly popular among those who emphasise the literal truth of the Christian Scriptures and who claim to uphold the traditional faith of Christians. Recent years have seen a new confidence and indeed numerical growth in those who profess an evangelical faith of this kind: and in the Roman Catholic church a 'conservative' tendency under the present Papacy has also led many in this direction.

On the other hand there are Christians who argue that claims for God's real existence are misleading and it should be accepted that the word 'God' stands for no more than a human ideal, perhaps of goodness, justice, truth or beauty. Such a view is espoused by the Sea of Faith network, which takes its name from television broadcasts delivered by the theologian, Don Cupitt, subsequently published with the same name. The network provides a booklet to explain its concerns from which I quote:

> In *Taking Leave of God* ... 1980, Cupitt argued that 'an objective metaphysical God is no longer either intellectually secure nor even morally satisfactory as a basis for spiritual life'. Instead 'faith in God must be understood as expressing an autonomous decision to

pursue the religious ideal for its own sake'. Theological realism –
belief in an objectively 'real' God, somehow outside and independent of human consciousness – had to be replaced by a free,
agnostic faith – with no certainties and no guarantees.[1]

Between realist and non-realist, there is not only a dispute about
the reality of God, but also about the nature of theological truth. In
talking of God are we dealing with factual certainties, or are we
merely expressing our own outlook on life? One writer, Jerome
Bertram, has used the term 'Dogmatical' for the first position and
'Liberal' for the second.[2] The dogmatical sees talk of God as factual;
the liberal sees it more as fictional – if it is true, it is in the sense one
might speak of poetical truth.

This classification is useful but it needs to be handled carefully.
Some who in general might be called liberal Christian thinkers have
their own dogmatical side. For example, they may dismiss angels and
demons, the Devil, miracles and the Virgin Birth and much else as
fictions: but their purpose is to define a core of faith which is credible
to the modern mind. This core is then held to be factually true. I
shall refer to this pruning away as a reductionist tendency, because it
reduces the contents of the faith. Reductionism may go all the way
with the Sea of Faith movement, or it may stop at a certain point and
declare that here at last is left a hard residue of truth which may be
held with certainty.

Another approach to truth is what might be called the confessional
stance. The believer witnesses to what for him or her is true, but does
not necessarily claim that this is a universal, factual kind of truth: it
is simply what he or she feels compelled by faith and experience to
declare. This approach allows the commitment faith has generally
valued, without demanding certain knowledge of things unknowable.
It might be expressed in simplest form by the assertion, 'I don't know
if it's true for others, but I know it is true for me.' Much modern
theology has elements of both reductionist and confessional
approaches and it would not be profitable to assign writers simplisti-
cally to one or other category.

The nature of theological truth is not a matter for theologians or
philosophers alone. It faces every Christian who thinks about faith,
or who faces questions about it. Is there really a God? Do you believe
in life after death? Did the resurrection actually happen? For most
believers there are matters about which they tend to offer reductionist answers, and other matters about which they want to be
'dogmatical', and there may will be 'confessional' aspects as well.

Outside the churches there are many who wrestle with such questions. Unable to accept what may seem like 'fairy stories', they may

still harbour beliefs about God, prayer, the after-life and so forth. There are also many seeking something deeper in life than a superficial materialism, yet who lack the language to define it. To these the 'dogmaticals' may seem to know too much about what is intrinsically unknowable, and to know it in too much detail. Yet it may seem that the reductionists have watered down what attracts because of its mystery, the impossibility of explaining it – and the non-realists have explained it away altogether. The attraction of religion is that it attempts to speak of the transcendent, that which is beyond human knowing: too much certainty is incredible, too much explaining away is in the end uninteresting.

Art, music, poetry, depth of human relationship, the beauty of nature, personal introspection, have for very many elicited a sense of something beyond the rational, the explicable, the comprehensible. Religion has claimed a place in this company, indeed a central place, for it offers a language by which such transcendental experiences may be held in memory, meditated upon, ordered and made mutually coherent: related also to more ordinary matters, expressed in rational and moral values, pursued as a comprehensive goal of living.

Traditionally, in the language of the Christian religion, the word 'God' has been indispensable to this enterprise. The concept which it encodes is, however, notoriously elusive, indeed, more than elusive, since God is generally held to be inconceivable. Crude conceptions of God repel those who might otherwise be able to relate their transcendental experiences to the Christian faith. Yet the residue of history is such that crude conceptions abound. I have already mentioned John Robinson's *Honest to God*.[3] His call to abandon images of God as either above a flat earth or outside a round earth scandalised many in the churches. Peculiarly, non-churchgoers also were upset, unwilling to lose their image of the God in whom perhaps they did not believe. Robinson called for an image of God in the depths of human life: one, therefore, which might relate to transcendental experience. About the positive content of this image he offered little more. The impact of his book, however, revealed the enormous gap between the popular notion of God and what the theologians of the past had written. Robinson was often said to be paraphrasing the work of the German theologians of the twentieth century, men such as Tillich and Bultmann. His point however was not a new one. The fourteenth-century author of *The Cloud of Unknowing*[4] also warned against looking for a God 'up there', and in the great tradition of theology from the fourth-century fathers through the mediaeval scholastics and beyond very sophisticated philosophical discussions of the 'nature' of God will be found. In such, a geographical locating of God has no place.

The nearest that traditional theology came to a description of God is in the delineation of the divine Attributes: eternity, infinity, ubiquity, ineffability, omnipotence, omniscience and others. I begin now with some thoughts about eternity.

The kind of experiences to which I have referred – of transcendence, of a depth beneath the surface of things – are often said to have a timeless quality. In the peerless prose of Thomas Traherne, the seventeenth-century writer, an experience from his childhood is described in such terms:

> The Corn was Orient and Immortal Wheat, which never should be reaped, nor was ever sown. I thought it had stood from Everlasting to Everlasting.
>
> The Dust and Stones of the Street were as Precious as GOLD. The Gates were at first the End of the World, the Green Trees when I saw them first through one of the Gates Transported and Ravished me; their Sweetnes and unusual Beauty made my Heart to leap, and almost mad with Extasie, they wer such strange and Wonderful Things: The Men! O what Venerable and Reverend Creatures did the Aged seem! Immortal Cherubims! And yong Men Glittering and Sparkling Angels and Maids strange Seraphick Pieces of Life and Beauty! Boys and Girles Tumbling in the Street, and Playing, were moving Jewels. I knew not that they were Born or should Die. But all things abided Eternally as they were in their Proper Places. Eternity was Manifest in the Light of the Day, and som thing infinit Behind evry thing appeared: which talked with my Expectation and Moved my Desire.[5]

Traherne described such experiences as made of 'Pure and Virgin Apprehensions, which I had in my Infancy'.[6] To know God, he urges, is to regain such experiences and to see the world once more with the uncorrupted eye of a little child. Timelessness is an essential quality of such experience and, if so broad and ill-defined a category as that of transcendental experience could be given definition, it would need to include a reference to it: a transcendental experience is one in which 'time stands still'.

There are many grounds upon which belief in God may be based, and experience is only one of them. However, without experience of God belief in him is an arid business and I hazard the view that for most believers it is some sort of transcendent experience which gives life to their belief.[7] Such moments open us to what almost inevitably we call 'the eternal' , 'the infinite', or the mystical.

For this reason, rather than for philosophical reasons, the attribution of eternity to God seems demanded by popular experience. A god who was not, in Eliot's words 'the still point of the turning world',[8] would be merely another contingent thing, a piece of cosmic furniture.

Christian philosophers have had philosophical reasons for ascribing eternity to God. These reasons are generally less persuasive, I suggest, than the experiences I have written of, but they result in descriptions which may well articulate those experiences.

For example, Thomas Aquinas wrote:

> Boethius defined eternity as the instantaneously whole and complete possession of endless life. We derive this idea of eternity by contrasting it with time, which, as Aristotle says, measures before and after in changes. An unchanging thing displays no before and after, nor does it begin or end. So we call it eternal meaning that it itself is endless, without beginning or end, and that the eternity which measures it has no before and after but is instantaneously whole.[9]

And again more briefly:

> Just as the notion of time starts from the notion of the present moment as passing, so the notion of eternity starts from the idea of an instant that abides.[10]

The eternal is changeless and indivisible. It is all wholly present. It is therefore not the same as the everlasting. As Aquinas put it,

> Time differs from eternity not primarily because it begins and ends (for conceivably the heavens might go round and round for ever), but because it measures changes whereas eternity is an instantaneous whole measuring abiding existence.[11]

I propose to juggle with this concept for a little, following the same logic as Aquinas. The everlasting is not as such eternal since it is in time, indeed in all of time. While the everlasting is not the same as the eternal, yet among temporal things the everlasting most nearly expresses the eternal. It provides the closest image of the timeless within time. Hence God, described by creatures of time, is called everlasting, though strictly he is more than that, he is eternal. Traherne, describing a glimpse of eternity in the passage I have quoted above, called the corn everlasting. That which is everlasting but not eternal, is unchanging, but it is not instantaneously whole. Only its present existence is present, its future and past, though just like its present are not present. The everlasting is thus an image of the eternal in time. It is as near as time can come to displaying timelessness. The ultimate conception of timelessness is the eternal and I shall therefore call the everlasting a *penultimate* form of timelessness.

Everlastingness is not the only penultimate form. Another is the momentary, that which exists only for a moment. For such a thing is instantaneously whole and unchanging – it has no time in which to change. It is not there – it is there in its fullness – and it is gone again. Such a thing is not subject to the processes of becoming and of passing away, which determine the life of most things. The momentary is not the same as the eternal because obviously the eternal is always there and always will be, but when the momentary is there, it is instantaneously whole. In contrast what least expresses eternity is something that comes to be for a time, and changes, and passes away, the life of a flower, or a beast, or even a human being. As a psalm often used in funerals puts it:

> The days of man are but as grass: for he flourisheth as a flower of the field. For as soon as the wind goeth over it, it is gone: and the place thereof shall know it no more. But the merciful goodness of the Lord endureth for ever and ever... .[12]

My juggling has been conducted in the framework of scholastic philosophy. It is not mere logical juggling, however, since it reflects something of those experiences which may be called transcendent. Such experiences are generally fleeting. While the heavens may open and eternity be glimpsed, yet the disclosure is only for a few moments. The impact of it may, nevertheless, last a life-time, and through it a whole world of meaning may be bestowed.

Boethius' eternity is a paradoxical combination of the endless and the instantaneously whole. Either side of the paradox, the everlasting or the momentary, may be expressions in time of the eternal. A glimmer of eternity is often experienced too in the face of that which is very old, whose beginning is lost in the mists of time, the ancient and the ageless, for these approximate in feeling to the everlasting. 'She is older than the rocks among which she sits', wrote Walter Pater of Leonardo da Vinci's *Mona Lisa* and thereby hinted at the essence in her of the eternal Mother. God himself is called in Scripture *the Ancient of Days*.[13] Likewise eternity is expressed in the very new, the new-born, in that which happens for the *first* time. Such things have no history, exist in no definite span of time and so in some degree express the eternal. We encounter them in the instant of their appearing. Thus the evangelists describe Jesus on the first Palm Sunday entering Jerusalem on *a colt which no one has yet ridden*.[14] The otherwise insignificant detail hints at an eternal weight of significance. Again after the Crucifixion Jesus is buried in a tomb

where no one had ever yet been laid.[15] Both tomb and donkey enter the
pages of the Gospel, as it were, fresh from the eternal source of being.

Eternity is likewise suggested by the last event of a series. An aging
travel-writer who had long before visited many places for the first
time, and returned often, found a renewed significance in returning
once more deliberately *for the last time.* Places regained the freshness
of the *first* visit. In the same spirit the last words of the dying may be
seen as a key to an understanding of a whole life. The last of the
series completes the picture, ends the story, and thus hints at the
instantaneous wholeness of eternity.

The uniting of old and new, or first and last, emphasises this
quality. The enthroned Christ of the book of Revelation announces
himself as *The First and the Last*[16] and the Lord God himself is *Alpha
and Omega,*[17] the beginning and the end. St Augustine addressed
God as 'Thou Beauty, both so ancient and so new',[18] an expression
of eternity which plucks at a deep unconscious chord in us.

To anticipate later discussion, eternity is expressed very strongly
in stories of the beginning and the end, the first times and the last
times, the Garden of Eden, the Celestial City. Such are the appropriate settings for stories of eternal significance, the stages upon
which are enacted the great myths of humankind.

A spectrum may be perceived, which I tabulate more fully at the
end of this chapter: first, the eternal in itself beyond time; second, the
eternal-within-time: third, the purely temporal. The eternal-within-
time includes the two penultimate forms of the everlasting and the
instantaneous. It includes too what we might call ante-penultimate
forms, the ancient and the untouched new, the first and the last. This
list is not an exclusive one. The transcendent may appear in an innu-
merable diversity of situations. However, the 'philosophical juggling'
reflects something of the actual experience of transcendence in so far
as it has a temporal location. Each of the components of the definition of eternity with which we began has the power to give strong
hints of it – the instantaneous and the endless.

We have discussed timelessness or eternity so far from the
perspective of Christian philosophy. The origins of this lie partly in
Plato, in Aristotle and in later Hellenistic metaphysics. They lie too
in the language of the Scriptures. A third influence is the Christian
mystical tradition through which experience irrigated the apparent
aridity of metaphysical argument. Thomas Aquinas himself was no
mean mystic and his speculative thought is inseparable from his
journey in prayer. He eventually esteemed his own vast output of
words to be of no value compared with silence before God.

Timelessness has featured also in an apparently quite different
area, the metapsychology of Sigmund Freud. Metapsychology is a

term used to describe the theory underlying the practice of psycho-analysis and therefore the description of the Unconscious is an important part of it. Freud attributed to the Unconscious five major characteristics, all of which I shall discuss. The first of these characteristics is that of timelessness.

> The processes of the Unconscious system are timeless; i.e. they are not ordered temporally, are not altered by the passage of time; they have no reference to time at all. Reference to time is bound up, once again, with the work of the Conscious system.[19]

From a Freudian perspective, glimpses of eternity, whatever else they are, are glimpses into the Unconscious. Transcendental experience is ordinary apprehension gilded by unconscious process. Freud himself discussed mysticism in 'Moses and Monotheism'[20] and his conclusions are summarised by Ernest Jones as follows:

> He accounted for this [i.e., that 'religious emotion attains a greater sublimity, profundity, and majesty than any other human emotion'] by pointing out that it represents a re-emergence, after a long period of latency, from the very depths of the Unconscious characterised by just those extremes of feeling that are inaccessible except in religious transformation.[21]

The Unconscious is the source of all emotion, in Freudian theory. Anything emerging from it comes with powerful feeling. In a transcendental moment an apparently commonplace sight or sound or smell is suddenly charged with an unexpected, often overwhelming significance. We may surmise that something has 'engaged the attention' – to use a paradoxical phrase – of the Unconscious and thus caused an outburst of otherwise unaccountable feeling.

Freud's Unconscious has been widely perceived as a dark cellar full of unpleasant contents. There is certainly an emphasis in his writing on the Unconscious as the source of mental illness, since he was first and foremost a doctor. The quotation above (and others) shows that for him the Unconscious is also a source of emotions displaying sublimity, profundity and majesty. Unfortunately he wrote very much less about this, and still less about its implications for religion and philosophy. One statement suggests that he was aware of the momentous possibilities that his theory was opening:

> At this point I shall venture to touch for a moment upon a subject which would merit the most exhaustive treatment. As a result of certain psycho-analytic discoveries, we are today in a position to

embark on a discussion of the Kantian theorem that time and
space are 'necessary forms of thought'. We have learnt that unconscious mental processes are in themselves 'timeless'. This means
in the first place that they are not ordered temporally, that time
does not change them in any way and that the idea of time cannot
be applied to them.[22]

This tantalising beginning is never developed by Freud, but we may
deduce that for Freud the timelessness of the unconscious had philosophical implications. Therefore it is not an abuse of his thinking to
develop it in that direction. Furthermore we have noted his respectful
account of religious feelings, feelings that, like all emotion, come
from the Unconscious. The enterprise that suggests itself therefore is
to present an understanding of the eternal God by means of the more
philosophical aspects of Freud's thinking.

In doing this we shall get little help from Freud's own account of
God. In 'The Future of an Illusion'[23] he identifies God with a
despotic aspect of the Super-ego, an internal and destructive tyrant.
This may have accurately reflected his own experience of the concept
of God, but such a concept is not that of orthodox Christian
theology. Instead, I shall argue that the concepts of God and of the
Unconscious have much in common. Timelessness is the first of five
aspects which they share. Experiences of timelessness are attributed
by the Christian to the influence of God, and by the psychoanalyst to
that of the Unconscious. This suggests that metapsychology and
theology have insights to offer one another. The benefit for theology
is that an explanation of what the word 'God' means becomes
possible, in terms which very many in the modern world understand
– terms derived from the Freudian revolution in humanity's understanding of itself.

Of course, concepts arising in different areas cannot simply be
equated without some alteration and even distortion.
Communication between two parties changes both. There will be
friends of each who do not like such change. Some in the analytic
tradition dislike loose talk of 'the Unconscious', preferring to speak
only of unconscious processes. Such will criticise my approach for
giving too much 'substance' to the Unconscious. On the theological
side some will criticise my account of God as giving him too little
'substance'. Nevertheless, my hope is that others will find the process
illuminating. An image of God will emerge which incorporates much
that Freud discovered about the Unconscious and which I believe
may open the language of faith to those at present bemused by it. I
hope, too, that this image will deliver those who cling to the language
of faith with difficulty from some of their doubts about it – doubts

particularly about what it means to say that God is a 'real being', intervenes in the world's affairs, and gives life to the dead. The traditional language of the church is not to be taken literally and I hope to open more flexible ways of understanding and professing it.

Table 1.1 Timelessness

Ultimate form:
The Eternal

Penultimate forms:
The Everlasting
The Momentary

Ante-penultimate forms:
The Coincidence of First and Last
The Ancient
The New

2   The Freudian Revolution

Copernicus is credited with the discovery that the earth is not the centre of the universe, but revolves around the sun, an insight that has changed humanity's image of itself ever since. A comparable overturning of the established frame of thought was brought about by Darwin. Humanity was not a uniquely privileged separate creation of God, but had descended from the apes. Humanity, therefore, could not as of right claim a central place even upon the earth, that Copernicus had already demoted. A third and comparable revolution may be attributed to Freud through his discovery that we, in our conscious selves, are not even at the centre of our selves, but dominated by the hidden and inaccessible world of the Unconscious. Freud himself certainly believed that his discoveries would be the basis of just such a third revolution in humanity's understanding of itself. In an essay published in 1917,[1] he argued that psychology was inflicting a third wound to human pride, comparable to the cosmological and biological blows already delivered by science.

Both the Copernican and Darwinian revolutions administered a severe shock to the religious understanding of the day. At the time theologians opposed them furiously, while after a period of reflection later theologians attempted to rescue faith from the challenge presented to it, and even to incorporate the new discoveries as insights into the working of God. The language of the Scriptures was at odds with both and, to this day, the teaching of evolution is banned in schools by many of the states of the supposedly most advanced nation upon earth. Flat-earthers, still troubled by Copernicus, are less prominent. When, however, John Robinson wrote *Honest to God* in 1962,[2] suggesting that God was not seated above the clouds, there was an outcry from the churches to which even the learned Michael Ramsey, Archbishop of Canterbury, subscribed.[3] Robinson was certainly not the first theologian to take account of Copernicus, but the religious imagery dear to the faithful had still not fully adjusted to the consequences of his discovery.

It is therefore not wholly surprising that although the Freudian revolution began a hundred years ago, faith has not yet come to terms with it, and theology has not absorbed, still less, exploited it. The 'wound to human pride' was intensified by Freud's fierce attack on religion in *The Future of an Illusion*.[4] Furthermore, priests and pastors as 'doctors of the soul', have felt supplanted by a new and often hostile expertise. Conscience and good will reinforced by divine grace seem inadequate guides to moral choice in a post-Freudian world, which has knowledge of the power of unconscious guilt and its origins in sexual pathology.

For these and other reasons Freud's discovery of the unconscious world has seldom been positively used by theology. Perhaps there has been a fear that everything will be reduced to sex, a subject the churches have always found threatening.

Sexual forces were indeed credited by Freud with much power, and he saw them as the predominant influence in the origin of mental illness. Yet he did not see sexual libido as the only human drive and, from the earliest years, some of his followers, notably Jung and Adler, founded movements which emphasised other primary sources of human motivation. Even within the Freudian movement a relatively close adherent, Ian Suttie,[5] argued that love was a more fundamental human drive even than sex. More influential than he, Melanie Klein made the bond between mother and child the focus of her attention and many others since, while retaining the fundamental distinction between conscious and unconscious, have explained human behaviour in ways more various than permitted by narrow Freudian orthodoxy. The British Psycho-analytic Society, for example, divides itself into Contemporary Freudian, Kleinian and Independent sectors, each embracing considerably different theories. To follow Freud in his understanding of the make-up of the human mind as both conscious and unconscious does not mean subscribing to a single theoretical model, still less is it to believe that the sexual drive is supreme.

Analysts of all traditions deal with the most powerful and fundamental feelings to which humanity is subject. Overwhelming guilt and fear, devastating anxiety, tremendous anger, but also great warmth and love, excitement, wonder and delight may break out in analytic sessions. These are manifestations of what Freud called 'primary process', in contrast to the milder thoughts and feelings of 'secondary process'. Primary process is the world of the infant and the child is still open to it, but by adulthood it has become largely inaccessible and buried. Nevertheless, it continues to dominate conscious emotional life and the fundamental values of the adult come from its influence, however much they may be wrapped in rational thinking.

Primary process breaks through to consciousness, not only in analysis, but through art, drama, poetry, in great passion of any kind, and in what I have called transcendental experience. If theology does not take account of these things it is flat and sterile: if it does not understand them in some way – and why not Freud's, since many do? – it risks being at the mercy of pathological distortion, as conspicuously in its witch-huntings, its inquisitions and its support of tyrannies, it has been.

Furthermore, and this is the most important point, God is known most intimately within ourselves, as the soul of our soul, as that in which we live and move and have our being. If Freud has any truth to tell about the soul, then there is something to be learnt from him too about 'the soul of the soul'.

When we turn to Freud's writings we find a wide range from description of practical technique to general reflections upon the nature of humanity. He may be seen in two lights: as a therapist or as a philosopher. His legacy to therapy has been the subject of as many divisions and dissensions as perhaps the legacy of Christ, a few of which have been referred to already. The present state of that legacy requires a brief discussion at this point.

The official custodian is the International Psycho-analytic Society, represented in many nations by a national society. To qualify for membership it is necessary to undergo a full analysis, at the hands of an authorised training analyst.

A full analysis is lengthy procedure requiring very frequent sessions for a period of years. In these sessions the analysand will talk freely of his or her problems and of the emotional occurrences of life. The analyst may say little, but the aim is to direct attention to recurring emotional patterns which relate to very early experience. Many, or most, emotional difficulties are caused by events, or even mere thoughts, the memories of which have been buried in the Unconscious. They are 'repressed', and there is a powerful resistance to their emergence. A major part of the analyst's task is to enable the analysand to overcome this resistance. In the course of time a 'transference relation' is established in which the analyst takes the place of the parent or other significant figure in the real or imagined events of which the memories have been repressed. Buried emotions may then come to the surface and it may be possible to face the thoughts which resistance has kept hidden.

The technique of analysis commands general support from members of the Society. However, the theories of the mind that analysts employ are far more diverse. Few are still bound by the whole panoply of theory as Freud left it. Most are in practice guided by understandings drawn from a variety of sources and not many subscribe to some one, overarching theoretical model. The Freudian world is a community with a common language, but without a single common theory. It does not now, as once it did when Freud's own influence was dominant, have the intellectual unity of most branches of science.

From the outside there is a mounting criticism of the claims of psychoanalysis and psychotherapy which has been given impetus by bitter disputes over accusations of child abuse based upon the alleged recovery of buried memories. As there have been from Freud's time, there are behaviourist psychologists who contest the existence of the Unconscious, or at least the validity of the analytical approach to it. A new threat is posed by advances in neurology which some believe may ultimately give physical access to mental processes to an extent so far only dreamed of, and might conceivably leave analysis in a backwater wedded to the Cartesian separation of mind and body. The therapeutic aspect of Freud's legacy, while very much alive, seems to the outsider to be facing challenges both from within (in terms of coherence) and from without. Whereas the giant figures of its past were widely read by the general public, it has now become a more specialist world. Yet its subject matter – the depths of the human soul – remains of the most vital importance to us all, and it still has much to impart about it.

A very different assessment may be made of what Freud bequeathed to philosophy. The *Shorter Oxford English Dictionary* offers nine main definitions of the word 'philosophy', some of which are sub-divided. Of these two are now rare or only occasionally used. The original and widest meaning is given as 'The love, study, or pursuit of wisdom, or of knowledge of things and their causes, whether theoretical or practical.' Another, qualified as 'moral' philosophy, is 'The knowledge or study of the principles of human action or conduct.' Yet another is, 'The system which a person forms for the conduct of life.' All these may be contrasted with what is called 'now the most usual sense': 'That department of knowledge or study which deals with ultimate reality, or with the most general causes and principles of things.' Academic philosophers in Britain have largely worked in the area of the last definition, and, under the influence of linguistic philosophy, in a restricted space within that. Freud's influence there is certainly limited, even barely detectable. The situation is different elsewhere, and in France for instance, Lacan, an intellectual descendent of Freud, has great influence in both psychoanalytic and academic philosophical circles. It is, however, Freud's legacy to the general public that I want to emphasise. I suggest that if there is a popular 'philosophy' at the end of the twentieth century it is loosely speaking of Freudian origin. I suggest that the ordinary person in the Western world believes in unconscious or subconscious influence and believes further that the springs of feeling and of conduct largely proceed from this. It is a suggestion that would take many pages to establish and I suspect they would be tedious pages. I intend to spare myself and the reader and proceed without fortifying the position adopted at this point. To those who wholly disagree this book will be pointless in any case, and the reader who even partially agrees may follow my argument without necessarily subscribing entirely to this view.

I claim that if there is a popular 'philosophy' in the sense of humanity's understanding of itself – in the Western world at this point of time – it is of loosely Freudian origin. The influence of his thinking is incontestably wider than such possible philosophical competitors as the linguistic school emanating from Wittgenstein, or the existentialists from Hegel and Sartre. Whatever their merits – and they are many – the great philosophers of the last half century have left relatively little mark beyond their own immediate academic circles and even a well-educated man or woman 'in the street' would be pressed to name more than a very few. Bizarre though it may be, astrologers and the Buddha have more influence than any of them upon human self-understanding and in that respect are Freud's nearest competitors.

The popular 'philosophy' deriving from Freud may be fragmentary, ignorant and ill-considered, yet its primary common feature is belief in the world of the Unconscious. Christian theology has seldom been ashamed to use the world's understanding of itself to express its faith in terms relevant and understandable to its market. Yet it is has made little use of Freud or Jung or those who descend intellectually from them.

The fourth-century fathers of Christian theology widely adopted Platonistic philosophy to expound the faith. St Thomas Aquinas in thirteenth-century Paris, inspired by the rediscovery of Aristotle, adopted his thinking for the same purpose. He spoke of turning the water of philosophy into the wine of faith. In the twentieth century Bultmann and Tillich, two of the greatest names in Protestant theology, have been deeply indebted to existentialism. So, too, have the Roman Catholic Karl Rahner and the Anglican John Macquarrie and both have exercised great influence in their communions. The philosophy of Whitehead gave birth, mainly in the United States of America, to a whole school of 'process theologians'. Most of the great philosophers have left their mark on theology somewhere and without their influence its history would be immeasurably the poorer.

Meanwhile Jung himself developed psychological insights into something very like a religious faith, claiming from them a certainty of God's existence greater than mere belief. Victor White, in his fascinating though sadly neglected book *God and the Unconscious*,[6] tried to baptise Jung fully into Roman Catholicism. Yet Freud, whose influence on the world is so immense, has been little used by theology, despite his influence in pastoral matters.

I propose then to attempt to sketch out how his legacy, a widespread popular philosophy of our time, might be of service to Christian orthodoxy. I believe the Chilean psychoanalyst, Ignacio Matte Blanco, has particularly opened the door to this possibility and it is to his theory that we shall shortly turn.

3   Matte Blanco and Symmetric Logic

Freud was born in 1864 and the basis of his revolution was laid before 1900. As a doctor and medical researcher he intended his work to be thoroughly founded on scientific principles. The science of his time had not yet been troubled by the discoveries of Einstein and Heisenberg.[1] Newtonian physics was the king of the sciences and there is no reason to doubt that Freud subscribed to the prevailing view. In principle the world was subject to an absolute mechanical determinism. If at one point of time the position, mass and velocity of every atom could be established, then theoretically the entire future of the world could be calculated exactly. No one of course believed that it was possible to do that calculation, but the principle of total scientific determinism seemed unchallengeable and to follow unquestionably from Newton's laws of motion. The central concept in this scheme was energy – the mass of an object multiplied by the square of its velocity.

Energy, doubtless because of the prevailing outlook, was also a central concept in the psychology of Pierre Janet, a leading figure of the time and a cardinal influence upon Freud.[2] When Freud began to describe the processes of the mind it was largely in terms of flows of energy attributable to certain drives or instincts. Although he did not attempt to connect these with observable impulses of any physical property, such as electricity, for example, he probably expected that at some distant future time that would be possible. Energy was the dominant scientific category and it was dominant also for Freud. Everything in principle could be reduced to it.

The twentieth century has transformed the simplicities of Newtonian physics. The atom long ago was imagined as like a minute billiard ball. It then became something like a miniature planetary system composed of subatomic particles. These in turn soon ceased to be predictable minute objects and became the probabilities of an occurrence which, according to Heisenberg, could never be wholly determined. Meanwhile the solid certainty of Newtonian mass dissolved and under Einstein mass became another form of energy into which it might be transformed through nuclear reaction. The models used by scientists for both the very small and the very large have become quite unlike things which we encounter in ordinary living and behave in ways apparently counter to common experience. To describe these models the language of science has become paradoxical and complex in a way inconceivable to the nineteenth-century physicist.

In the twentieth century logic and language have been subject to a new scrutiny. In philosophy, particularly that of Wittgenstein, it has become apparent that language does not always do what it might at first appear to be doing. Apparently self-evident truths no longer yield other truths by processes of simple deduction. Language, and the models we draw from it, are more complicated and slippery than once was assumed. Logic is no longer utterly clear and self-authenticating. Thought has to be self-examining and turned in upon its own mechanisms of language and of logic in a way that once it was not.

Psychoanalysis might almost be called the study of human irrationality, yet it was not until the Chilean psychoanalyst Ignacio Matte Blanco published *The Unconscious as Infinite Sets* in 1975[3] that sustained and systematic attention was given to the logic of the Unconscious. In this work energy is firmly displaced from its centrality and is replaced by logic. The possibility of a new coherence in psychological theory was opened. It is with the consequences of Matte Blanco's discovery that we shall be very largely concerned.

Matte Blanco[4] was born in 1908 in Chile and graduated in medicine at the University in Santiago. His interest soon turned towards psychiatry and particularly psychoanalysis, and this interest led him to London in the mid-1930s. One who wishes to be an analyst has first to be analysed, and this he undertook with Walter Schmideberg, a classical Freudian, and son-in-law of Melanie Klein (who herself was perhaps the most influential innovator among Freud's successors). Matte Blanco studied under many of the best-known analysts of the time, including Melanie Klein, Anna Freud, and Ernest Jones, founder of the British Psycho-analytic Society, and one of the first and most faithful disciples of Freud himself. Philosophy and mathematics had interested Matte Blanco from early days and in this period he was tackling the formidable work of Russell and Whitehead, *Principia Mathematica*, which, *inter alia*, attempts to solve the logical paradoxes thrown up by the mathematical concept of infinity. In 1940, he moved to America, and was employed first as a therapist and analyst at Johns Hopkins Hospital in Baltimore and subsequently at Duke University, North Carolina, and the Medical Center in New York. The great mathematician,

Courant, was then teaching at Columbia University, and Matte Blanco joined his famous weekly seminars to continue his studies in mathematical logic.

In 1948, Matte Blanco returned to his native land as Chair of Psychiatry at the University of Chile. His work with psychotic patients was particularly notable. Psychosis is a term that encompasses many of the most severe and disturbed forms of mental illness, those which the layman would identify as simply madness. In general it has been found almost inaccessible by psychoanalytic techniques. Yet it was these which most interested Matte Blanco.

A desire to follow his own developing theories led to a new departure in 1966. He moved to Rome as a training analyst – one responsible for analysing and training other analysts – and as Chairman of Psychiatry at the Catholic University of Rome also taught in the Postgraduate School there. In 1975 the fruits of a life-time's work – Matte Blanco was then aged sixty-seven – appeared in his profound book, *The Unconscious as Infinite Sets*. In 1988 a sequel was published, *Thinking, Feeling and Being*.[5] In 1990 an accident caused him severe brain damage and his health declined rapidly until his death in 1995. All his life he was a practising Roman Catholic.

It will be clear that Matte Blanco was, in several senses, a traveller. Geographically he worked in Chile, England, the United States, Chile again, and Rome. Linguistically he was at home in Spanish, English, Italian and familiar with other languages as well. Intellectually, he was trained as a doctor, and worked as a psychiatrist, while practising as a psychoanalyst, two areas not always held together. He had wide philosophical interests and an intense amateur interest in mathematics, which extended considerably beyond his main focus in logical theory. In his writings there are also occasional hints of an interest in theology.

The combination of mathematics and psychoanalysis at first sight seems unpromising. The one is regarded as highly rational, precise and impersonal; the other as in each respect the reverse.[6] The genius of Matte Blanco was to bring the two together creatively, and doubtless his multi-lingual, multi-cultural and multi-disciplinary experience was necessary for this achievement. Before embarking on the detail of his theories, a few preliminary remarks may help particularly the reader for whom mathematics is unknown and threatening territory.

In psychosis, a term which embraces schizophrenia and paranoia, concepts are used in irrational and apparently chaotic ways. It was in dealing with psychotic patients that Matte Blanco found the germ of his theory of the 'logic' of the Unconscious. He believed – or discovered – that the apparent irrationality of his patients was not a wholly arbitrary chaos, but one that exhibited certain patterns. It was a *patterned* irrationality. He described it as an alternative, and bizarre, logic. The basis of this pattern was symmetry, in a particular mathematical sense.

MATHEMATICAL SYMMETRY

The non-mathematician may think of symmetry as primarily a visual, geometrical matter – left corresponding to right, for example. But even at a quite elementary level of mathematics the word is also used algebraically. If, for example, in the statement of a problem two terms, a and b, are present in the same way, then it may be said there is a symmetry between them: and then there must also be the same symmetry in the solution of the problem. If they are interchangeable in the statement of the problem, they must be interchangeable in its solution. For example, consider this problem:

Given the equation

$$a^2 + 2ab + b^2 = c^2,$$

if a,b and c are positive numbers, express in simplest form the relationship between them.

It is obvious that if a and b are interchanged, the equation is unaltered. There is symmetry therefore between a and b in the statement of the problem.

The solution to the problem, as the mathematical will realise, is as follows:

$$a^2 + 2ab + b^2 = (a + b)^2$$

So we have $(a + b) = c$ (the alternative of $-c$ is excluded since all are positive) and therefore $a + b = c$.

As we would hope, a and b are interchangeable in the answer. Wrong answers such as $a - b = c$, or $a + 2b = c$ can be seen to be wrong because interchanging a and b in them produces different formulae: $b - a$ is not the same as $a - b$, nor is $b + 2a$ the same as $a + 2b$. In the wrong answers there is an asymmetry between a and b, which immediately proves they cannot be right.

The words 'symmetry' and 'asymmetry' in Matte Blanco, and in this book, are to be understood in this mathematical sense. Included in the meaning of symmetry is the idea that one thing is interchangeable with another: and in asymmetry is the idea that they are not interchangeable.

INFINITE EMOTION

A second observation that Matte Blanco made about psychotic patients was that their emotions seemed to be raised to an infinite pitch. They did not feel anything in a moderate or containable degree: fear, anger, love or hate appeared without limit, or not at all. This infinity of emotion seemed at the root of their problems, creating havoc in their lives. Matte Blanco was aware from Russell and Whitehead that infinity was at the root of the problems of fundamental mathematics, where it seemed that it played havoc with the normal behaviour of numbers.

If we put together these two ideas of symmetry and infinity we perceive something of the 'reasoning' of the psychotic. For instance, if one finds another person threatening, normal reasoning and experience will appropriately limit the degree of threat in the situation. But a psychotic may perceive that person as interchangeable with any other person who has ever threatened them, or ever might threaten them, or with any threat they may ever have dreamed of. Thereby the threat becomes limitless or infinite. The madness of the psychotic can therefore be seen as expressed, perhaps even rooted, in a misuse of symmetry – in the mathematical sense. The psychotic sees symmetry where the normal person does not and, thereby, emotion is inflated to an infinite extent.

SAMENESS AND DIFFERENCE

In Britain Matte Blanco's thinking has been most prominently championed by Eric Rayner, a well-known British psychoanalyst. His book, *Unconscious Logic*,[7] is a relatively simple exposition of these theories. Rayner expounds symmetry and asymmetry in terms of the basic need of any animal to find its way around its environment. It is important to be able to discriminate one thing from another; something good to eat, for example, from something poisonous. This *discrimination of difference*, as Rayner calls it, is vital to life. It requires an awareness of *asymmetry* – that some things are not interchangeable with each other.

It is also vital, however, to recognise some things as essentially the same as others; to recognise one apple (something good to eat) as essentially the same as another, which may also therefore be trusted not to be poisonous. *The registration of sameness* is as vital to life as the awareness of difference, for without it memory would have no purpose, and experience bring no benefit. The registration of sameness is similar to the recognition of symmetry (one thing may be interchanged with another). The discrimination of difference corresponds to the recognition of asymmetry. The psychotic paranoid who responds to a small slight as though it were a murderous assault is unable to discriminate difference. Instead he or she registers any hostility as of the same degree and identifies it with every other possible or imagined hostile act, so that the degree becomes infinite.

SYMMETRY AND THE UNCONSCIOUS

I can now conclude these preliminary remarks about symmetry and asymmetry with one more point. Matte Blanco believed that the Unconscious primarily uses symmetry, the registration of sameness and the ignoring of difference, whereas Consciousness primarily is used to discriminate differences. Thus the psychotic in situations that call for conscious discrimination acts under excessive unconscious influence.

For Matte Blanco the psychotic exposes to open view the workings of the Unconscious, what Freud called primary process and which he claimed was also revealed in dreams. Primary process has many strange features and Freud's findings may be summed up under five headings known as 'the five characteristics of the unconscious'. Matte Blanco was able to show that these five characteristics can be reduced to two general principles which are the foundations of his system. I shall now turn to these.

THE PRINCIPLE OF GENERALISATION

The first of these is the principle of generalisation. According to this the Unconscious does not relate to individuals, but only to 'classes' of which they are a member. An aggressive dog is felt to encompass the class of all dangerous aggressors – and thus is perceived as presenting an infinite threat. It is easy to see that irrational phobia is at once accounted for by this principle: something trivially alarming, or even just something connected with an alarming situation, is treated as though the whole class or category of alarming things is present in it. Similarly, someone 'head over heels' in love will see the loved person as having every possible lovable characteristic, not merely the characteristics that first evoked the infatuation.

According to this principle, the Unconscious, having first treated an individual as a class, tends to treat this class as the sub-class of a more general class, and so on and on to an unlimited extent. For example, an aggressive dog may first be registered as the class of all aggressive dogs. This is then registered as a sub-class of all aggressive mammals, and that in turn as a sub-class of all aggressive creatures of any kind. The Unconscious, having registered something as fearful or desirable, registers it is as the same as other fearful or desirable things, in an ever more inclusive circle. The individual who evokes a strong feeling, thus potentially evokes this feeling to an infinite extent.

To summarise, by the principle of generalisation an individual is identified with a class to which it is felt to belong, and a class is iden-tified with wider classes of which it is a sub-set.

The link with the mathematics of the infinite is created by this property of the Unconscious. A finite set, for example of numbers, can only be put in a one-to-one correspondence with a set of the same size – a 'one-to-one correspondence' means a correspondence in which each member corresponds to one and only one member of the matching set. A finite set therefore obviously cannot be in one-to-one correspondence with one of its own sub-sets – for a sub-set will have fewer members. However, apparently paradoxically, the opposite is true of an infinite set. For example, if we think of the set of positive whole numbers, 1, 2, 3 etc., this can be put in one-to-one correspondence with the set of even numbers. This may be done by matching each number (of the whole set) with its double. Thus 1 corresponds to 2, 2 to 4, 3 to 6, etc. In this correspondence each number has one and only one match. Therefore, speaking crudely, there seem to be as many even numbers as there are whole numbers altogether. Yet looked at in another way, again speaking crudely, one would be tempted to think there were twice as many whole numbers as whole even numbers! An infinite set therefore can be put in one-to-one correspondence with a sub-set of itself.

Matte Blanco noticed that much of the irrational thinking of the psychotic could be explained if one assumed that sub-classes were equated by it with wider classes of which they were a part: dangerous dogs were equated with aggressors of all kinds. This reminded him of the property of infinite sets described above. Having made this discovery about psychotics, he found it to be applicable too to all Unconscious thinking – in the sane as well as the mentally ill. Anyone acting under the dominance of the Unconscious thinks in a similar way. For example:

a mother who feeds belongs, let us say to the class of women who feed materially; a professor who teaches belongs to the class of men who feed mentally. When on account of a process of displace-ment an individual feels the professor as a mother who feeds he is, first of all treating both classes as subclasses of a more general class, that of those who feed ... The same thing can be seen to be true in any example of displacement .[8]

Displacement is one of the five characteristics Freud found in uncon-scious process and is a universal human phenomenon.

THE PRINCIPLE OF SYMMETRY

This first principle of Matte Blanco's, the principle of generalisation, is of great importance in his thinking. Yet more important is the second principle, the principle of symmetry, and with this principle we shall be much more engaged hereafter. The principle of symmetry is as follows:

> The system Unconscious treats the converse of any relation as identical with the relation. In other words, it treats asymmetrical relations as if they were symmetrical.[9]

To illustrate this first in an algebraic context – remembering that this notion of symmetry is a mathematical one – consider the simplest of all relations; for example, the equation $a = b$. It is a symmetrical relation between a and b, since interchanging a and b makes no difference to it: if $a = b$ then it is also true that $b = a$.

Contrast this with the relation $a > b$ (which means a is greater than b). This is not a symmetrical relation – because $b > a$ cannot be true as well. The relationship expressed by 'is greater than' is therefore an asymmetrical relation. Matte Blanco's second principle states that the Unconscious would treat such a relation as symmetrical and draw from $a > b$ the converse that also $b > a$, (despite this obviously being impossible in normal logic).

Most readers will probably find a less algebraic statement easier to understand. A proposition such as *John is the sibling of Mary* expresses a symmetrical relation, since in that case, clearly, it is also true that *Mary is the sibling of John*. By contrast, *John is the parent of Mary* expresses an asymmetrical relationship between John and Mary, since in that case clearly *Mary is the parent of John* cannot be true. Matte Blanco's second principle states that the Unconscious treats both as symmetrical, so that in this instance, to the Unconscious, if John is the parent of Mary, then also Mary is the parent of John.

This principle produces startling and irrational consequences. Common-sense reasoning is comprehensively violated. However, it does bring some order into irrationality. Whereas in all previous accounts of the workings of the Unconscious there is no systematic pattern to its irrationality, Matte Blanco provides a key by which this irrationality has a certain pattern. That pattern is the imposition of symmetry upon the asymmetrical.

Matte Blanco uses the term 'symmetric logic' to sum up his two principles, and in contrast the term 'asymmetric logic' to describe ordinary common-sense logic.

EMOTION AND SYMMETRY

It may seem that symmetric logic is found only in the world of madness. However that is very far from the case. The entire Freudian tradition affirms that all emotion is rooted in the Unconscious. Therefore any matter involving emotion is likely to be dealt with partially by symmetric logic. A commonplace illustration, which I borrow from Eric Rayner,[10] may help the reader to grasp this idea:

> An emotional and fond friend may feel something like this: 'Maisie's such a good friend to me' and then slip automatically into the thought, 'I'm her best friend', 'we're the best of friends'.

In this instance, emotion has first exaggerated a situation by the principle of generalisation – from 'a good friend' to 'the best of friends' – and then symmetry has imposed the deduction that because Maisie feels very warmly to her friend, her friend feels equally warmly to Maisie – yet the bitter reality very often is that this is not the case.

The stronger the emotion the more such 'symmetric deductions' are likely to occur. All too often one who is powerfully attracted to another sexually believes, contrary to the actual evidence, that the reverse must be the case. Tragically, this is often the logic of the rapist, who believes his victim must return his feelings, despite protests and struggles that in a more rational state would be reckoned as evidence to the contrary. Again, one who hates *has to believe* that his or her hatred is returned.

Many are the confusions in emotional situations that result from misreadings of the implicit logic. For example, two Indian brothers were sent to a boarding school in England. The younger felt very isolated and unhappy. Faithfully every week his mother wrote to each of them and on these letters his emotional security rested. Particularly important to him were her concluding words, 'with all my love'. However, one week his brother showed him the letter he had received, and to his dismay he found the same words at the end of his brother's letter too. 'How could both have *all?*', he asked himself. An understanding of the principle of generalisation might have saved him some of his pain, for if love is genuine, then some of it equates to all of it. Contrary to all conventional logic, two brothers can each have all their mother's love. It is intrinsically indivisible.

The contrast of the two logics may be illustrated by the vows in the Church of England's modern-language wedding service. Bride and groom both promise: *all that I have I share with you*. That is straightforward enough: bank accounts, material possessions of all sorts, and even time can be shared without violation of common-sense logic. But consider the next words of the vow: *all that I am I give to you*.

Thus first the groom gives himself to the bride. And then, after this, she gives herself back, in the same words, to the groom. The pedant, with the mind of the little boy in the last example, might conclude that she had returned what he had given her, and thus he ends up as two people, she as none. Such would hardly be the intention of the vows, nor the understanding of those who made them. Instances of this kind where symmetric logic is used without any sense of its illogicality may be endlessly multiplied.

It is by this same logic that the gift of the widow's mite is worth more than all the lavish donations of the rich. In the emotional realm the part is equal to the whole. The rich gave *some* of what they had: this might imply therefore that they have given all. But clearly they have not, for they have retained some (probably most) of what they have. Therefore emotionally they retained *all* of what they had – and so had not given at all. In contrast the widow retained nothing but gave *all* that she had.

Another often-told anecdote illustrates the contrast between asymmetric and symmetric thinking. A young man sent his girlfriend a letter:

I love you more than words can tell. I will climb every mountain to be with you and cross every ocean. Nothing will ever part us. I will bring you treasure from the ends of the earth and the pot of gold at the foot of the rainbow. I love you now and always and for ever.

He signed his name and added:

P.S. I will be at the bus-stop as usual on Sunday at 7 p.m., unless it's raining.

The letter takes every feeling to the infinite, expresses itself in impossible fantasy and claims all this for eternity. The message of the postscript is placed, dated and subject to the most unromantic limitation.

It is seldom that the territories of the symmetric and the asymmetric are so clearly separated as in this instance. More commonly emotional and personal matters are expressed in a blend which may take careful analysis to unravel. Even in dreams and in the utterances of the deeply disturbed patient there will be some asymmetric reasoning mingled with the symmetric 'reasoning' of the Unconscious.

THE CHARACTERISTICS OF THE UNCONSCIOUS AND SYMMETRY

Matte Blanco showed how his two principles accounted for the five main characteristics of unconscious process, as Freud described

them. These characteristics are as follows: timelessness, displacement, condensation, the non-contradiction of opposed impulses and,
lastly, the equivalence of fantasy and reality. I shall not repeat in full
the arguments given by Matte Blanco in *The Unconscious as Infinite
Sets* which justify the claim that his two principles explain these characteristics. In the case of timelessness, however, the argument is brief
and simple. If one event is before another, then the principle of
symmetry states that to the unconscious the second event is also
before the first. 'Before' and 'after' thus become meaningless – all
time is simultaneously present. To illustrate this one has only to
think of a dream in which one may simultaneously be in several
different periods of one's life at once – both at junior school for
instance, and in college and at work. This is the timelessness, or
eternity, of the Unconscious. It also illustrates Freud's condensation.
This characteristic describes how one person or one setting may
stand for many and inherit feelings appropriate to others. Thus the
work situation in the dream may be endowed with feelings originally
felt in a related situation at school. The Unconscious is treating both
situations as members of a class of similar situations, and because it
is not distinguishing them from one another, each may acquire
features drawn from the other. Displacement is a somewhat similar
phenomenon in which one person may evoke feelings felt in life
towards another – if one dreams of one's boss he may acquire
features of one's father, for example.

The characteristic of non-contradiction of opposed feelings means
that one can both love and hate, desire and fear the same person at
the same time, and the Unconscious seems not to register such as
opposites. The fifth characteristic, the equivalence of fantasy and
reality, means that to the Unconscious there is no distinction
between a memory of a real happening and the memory of a fantasy.
For example, if a child imagines some terrible happening in fantasy,
the memory of that fantasy is as real to the Unconscious as would be
the memory of a real event.

NON-CONTRADICTION AND SYMMETRY

We need to note an important aspect of Matte Blanco's treatment of
the non-contradiction of opposed impulses. To Freud this meant
that, for example, the Unconscious can wish simultaneously for both
the survival and the death of a terminally ill parent. In Consciousness
these not unnatural feelings will generally emerge one at a time – one
day the carer perhaps feels a longing for the prolongation of life, the
next that death may come quickly. Remembering the point that
Matte Blanco moves Freudian theory from a description of impulses

of energy towards a linguistic and logical account of the Unconscious, this characteristic becomes a propositional one. The Unconscious simultaneously holds both a proposition and, in a broad sense of the word, its contradiction. For example, *I wish he would recover* implies also *I wish he would die.*

Matte Blanco extends this characteristic beyond its source in impulses and wishes. For example, the unconscious belief that might be expressed as, '*I am all-powerful*', which is familiar in the phenomenon often underlying attitudes in the adult of infantile omnipotence, also implies the belief expressible as, '*I am totally powerless*'. Where the first belief is present, the second will, in general, be found to be present also. A thought in the Unconscious will imply an opposite thought as well.

Matte Blanco believed that his theory had simplified Freud's account of the Unconscious and given coherence to the five disparate characteristics that Freud had disclosed.

A REFORMULATION OF SYMMETRIC LOGIC

I shall now propound my own presentation of symmetric logic which, while in substance the same as Matte Blanco's, is intended to emphasise further the principle of symmetry and to display his logic more clearly as a system of logic.

As in common presentations of classical or common-sense logic, there are four main constituents. There are terms, which will be designated by capital letters: A, B, etc. Terms are the things about which something is said. What may be said about terms will be designated by small letters: p, q, etc. These two constituents together give propositions, p(A, B) for example means that something – p – is said about the terms A and B. For example if A and B are respectively John and Mary, and p is 'loves' then this means John loves Mary. Next there are logical connectors which relate propositions to one another: 'implies', 'not', 'and', 'therefore' and 'equals', for example. Finally there are the formal laws for manipulating propositions by means of the logical connectors.

We have already come across two of these formal laws. The first descends from Freud's non-contradiction of opposite impulses through Matte Blanco's translation of this to logic. It may be expressed as follows: p(A) *implies* not-p(A).

Any proposition about one term implies an opposite proposition about the same term. This is the law of opposition. For example *Mary loves* implies also *Mary hates*, producing the conclusion *Mary both hates and loves.*[11]

Another example has already been discussed: *I am powerful* implies *I am powerless*. Since in these cases the original proposition remains, so that *I am powerful* symmetrically implies *I am powerful and I am powerless*, the law of opposition may be more fully stated as: p(A) *implies* p(A) and not-p(A).

The next formal law has also already been encountered in Matte Blanco's principle of symmetry. I shall state it as follows: p(A,B) *implies* p(B,A) or, in fuller form, p(A,B) *implies* p(A,B) and p(B,A).

In words, any proposition about two terms implies a reflexive proposition in which the two terms exchange places. This is the law of reflection. For example, *Mary loves John* implies *John loves Mary*; or in the fuller version, *John and Mary love one another*. Or, as we have discussed, *Maisie is my best friend* implies *I am the best friend of Maisie*, giving the conclusion, *Maisie and I are each other's best friends*.

In common-sense logic (or asymmetric logic as Matte Blanco calls it), if the premises are true, so is the conclusion. We notice at once that that is not so in symmetric logic. Its deductions do not follow the path of fact, but of feeling or emotion.

There is another noteworthy difference. Asymmetric logic has a deterministic feel. That is to say it never delivers a new truth, though it may deliver truths that had not been clear before. Everything is already 'there' in the premises. It can only clarify or obfuscate what is already known. Symmetric logic, by contrast, has a considerable freedom. It may deliver falsehoods. It may also suggest truths not in any way apparent in advance, for unlike asymmetric logic it can move in a variety of directions. For example, *Maisie is my best friend*, as we have seen, can be treated as a two-term proposition about Maisie and me. However, it might also be treated as a one-term proposition just about Maisie. Then the first rule will deliver instead, *Maisie is my worst enemy*.

There are several ways of bringing negation into a one-term proposition. The verb may change into its opposite, so that *I like Maisie* might become *I dislike Maisie*. Or, more strangely, the object may take on negation, which delivers *I like not-Maisie*. At first sight *not-Maisie* seems meaningless: however, in mathematical set theory a similar usage suggests it should be understood as *everyone except Maisie*. So the full sentence is *I like everyone except Maisie*. In a similar way, the subject, in this case 'I', may take on the negation. This gives *Not-I* or *Everyone except me likes Maisie*.

It is clear that symmetric logic is a very peculiar logic, if it is one at all. I hope it is also clear that it lays bare a certain pattern in the flow of emotion, though more than one flow is possible from any given situation. These flows or changes in feeling are patterned by symmetry.

I have explained symmetry algebraically as the interchange of two terms. An image of this that some may find useful is of looking into a mirror. Left and right are interchanged: one's right eye, for example, is to the left of one's nose in the reflection. For an image of the one-term situation one may think of the symmetry between an object and its reflection in, for example, still water. If one looks down into a pool one sees the world stood on its head. A cloud high above one's head appears in the reflection down in the deepest depths: this may intuitively convey to some the symmetry of a proposition and its opposition.

Another example of how symmetric logic draws 'deductions' through these two laws may be helpful. A child grows up in fear of her father, which may be expressed by the proposition: *I am afraid of my father*. This looks like a two-term proposition about 'me' and 'my father'. The law of reflection then offers the deduction: *My father is afraid of me*, and the two together give, *My father and I are afraid of one another*.

Since symmetric logic has great freedom and is often interwoven with asymmetric logic, there are other possibilities. Starting again from *I am afraid of my father*, observation may add: *My father is a man*. The law of reflection deduces, *A – or any – man is my father*. Asymmetric logic then concludes: *I am afraid of any man (i.e. of all men)* – which is a common consequence of growing up in fear of one's father. But there are other ways the argument can proceed. *I am afraid of my father* might be treated as a one-term proposition, as though it were better expressed as: *My father is frightening*. The deduction, by the law of opposition might then be: *My father is safe*. This equates to: *I feel safe with my father* and, combining this with the starting point, we find: *I am both frightened by my father and feel safe with him*. This too is a possible consequence of living with a frightening father. It is mirrored in the religious field by the description of the numinous, the holy, as both terrifying and attractive.

A note of caution needs to be sounded to avoid misunderstanding. It is not claimed that the Unconscious constructs such arguments as those above in the step by step manner in which they have been expounded. Each step does not necessarily correspond to an equivalent unconscious process. On the contrary, the Unconscious is better thought of as reaching its conclusions in a single leap. However, the steps are means by which through considered use of symmetric and asymmetric logic, we may delineate the 'conclusions' to which the Unconscious may spring.

If one-term propositions are made symmetrical by 'opposition', and two-term by reflection, what of the three-term case? *Mary made friends with Maisie to spite Maude* might be an example of such a

proposition. Algebraically this may be written p(A,B,C). It is at once
clear that there is no single alteration that handles each of the three
terms in an equitable way. For example, p(B,A,C) has symmetrically
exchanged A and B, but has left C unaffected. The only way in which
mathematical symmetry can be preserved is by rotating the three
terms. If symmetry is applicable to a three-term proposition it can
only be as follows: p(A,B,C) implies p(A,B,C) and p(C,A,B) and
p(B,C,A). To change A,B,C to C,A,B the first letter has been moved
to second place, the second to third, and the third to first place. If the
same is done again we arrive at B,C,A – and, if we do it again, we will
have moved full circle and returned to A,B,C. Thus, by symmetry,
the single proposition p(A,B,C) delivers both itself and two new
propositions.

This third law of symmetric logic was not discussed by Matte
Blanco. It is, however, found in certain situations. For example, in
the interventions of social workers in situations of family violence,
the apparent situation is: *The social worker rescues a victim from a persecutor.* It has been persuasively argued[12] that such interventions are
often experienced in a complex way on three different levels. There
is first the plain fact that a victim is being rescued. However, all those
involved may experience the rescue emotionally as a persecution of
the actual persecutor: a new persecution from which the apparent
persecutor has to be rescued by the victim. Thus the rescuer has
become persecutor, the persecutor victim and the victim rescuer, and
one step of a rotation has taken place. Furthermore, the third implication is present at a still deeper emotional level. The social worker
may be working from his or her own sense of being a victim. The
underlying emotional truth then is that the victim is persecuting the
social worker by rousing this sense of 'being a victim'. The original
persecutor may then be seen as a rescuer because his or her actions
have enabled these inner feelings of victimisation to be acted out
vicariously and thereby projected and discharged. This may be
described as: *the persecutor rescues the rescuer from the victim.*

Whether this law of rotation throws light on the Oedipal triangle,
for example, I will leave the reader to explore: *The son kills the father
to possess the mother.* Rotation delivers: *The mother kills the son to possess
the father,* and: *The father kills the mother to possess the son.*

This example takes us into deep waters but certainly the shadow
of rotation seems to be cast over many situations: they are generally
made complex by the co-presence of two-term relationships between
the actors as well. For example, if *Mary makes friends with Maisie to
spite Maude,* it may be that concurrently, *Maude makes friends with
Mary to spite Maisie,* and *Maisie makes friends with Maude to spite
Mary.* However, there may be two-term relationships between

Maude and Mary, Mary and Maisie, and Maisie and Maude which overlie this simple pattern. Other relationships with fourth and further parties may further confuse the situation.

Theoretically, one could discuss four- and higher-term propositions also. However, although there are many situations which involve more than three people, it seems generally that there are not more than three distinct roles which they may each play in the same action. Two or more people will be found to be sharing a role, and therefore being encompassed by the same term, in such apparently larger situations. I shall therefore confine symmetric logic to three laws.

These laws express symmetry, but do they form a logic? Strictly speaking, a logician would probably argue that they did not. They violate one of the basic properties of logic, which is the distinction between true and false. Whatever is true is also false in symmetric logic. However, these rules do amount to a logic in the sense of a way of arguing, of deriving one proposition from another, and it is in that loose sense that the word is used by Matte Blanco and in this book.

In emotional situations people often argue 'falsely' by the criteria of common-sense logic. Matte Blanco's contention, which I follow, is that the workings of the Unconscious may be described by the assumption that it is operating by the rules of symmetric logic. This description is, of course, one made by the conscious mind and therefore more strictly it should be said that the workings of the Unconscious may be described from the perspective of consciousness *as though* it operated by the rules of symmetric logic. The pure Unconscious in itself is, I suppose, by definition utterly unknowable. To avoid verbosity, having made this disclaimer, I shall proceed as though the Unconscious does indeed follow these rules.

We come now to a very important and potentially confusing point in the argument of this book. We have been thinking of the unconscious and conscious aspects of the mind as though they were two clearly distinct entities. This model of the human mind goes back to the early work of Freud in which he writes of primary and secondary process, the former being the work of the Unconscious, the latter of Consciousness. In contrast to this model is the notion of a spectrum of mental states – at one end totally unconscious, at the other wholly conscious, and in between a gradation from one to the other. Thus a highly emotional and irrational state lies near to the unconscious, though with some conscious content also. And on the other hand the more matter-of-fact aspect of life is likely to be conducted with little unconscious interference though emotional values derived from the Unconscious may lie behind it. In Matte Blanco's second major work he describes five levels of mental functioning marked out by increasing degrees of unconscious thinking and of symmetric logic. The notion of a spectrum is of course common to many writers about the Unconscious and readers of Carl Jung will be particularly familiar with it. No one has devised a way of measuring the 'depth' of unconscious influence effectively and so the notion remains an intuitive one. Matte Blanco had hoped that he would provide such a measure but his work at that point remains incomplete and it seems clear that symmetric logic does not provide it for reasons that will now be discussed.

States of mind caused by paranoid schizophrenia are among the paradigms of unconscious functioning: they provided the impetus for much of Matte Blanco's discoveries as we have noted earlier. Symmetric logic is dominant and yet peculiarly it is not wholly dominant. To discuss this I shall borrow from Shakespeare's *A Midsummer Night's Dream* the thought that 'strong imagination' leads one to suppose that every bush is a bear.[13] Such a fear is typical of the paranoid state, and it is encompassed by symmetric logic. *Some bush-like things are bears*, therefore *Every bush-like thing is a bear* – the principle of generalisation. Yet there is asymmetry. The proposition *This bush is dangerous*, yields by symmetry *This bush is safe*. In the paranoid state that further extension of symmetric logic is not pursued. Again, if every bush has the properties of a bear, then what we might call bear/bushes ought also to have the properties of a bush: thus sometimes real bears would be perceived as bushes. What in fact the paranoid state involves is a selective use of symmetry limited by a definite asymmetry – a preference for attributing danger rather than safety in this case. The conclusion therefore is that the very unconscious state of paranoia includes also a residue of very firm asymmetry.

Matte Blanco equated the degree of unconscious influence with the degree to which symmetric logic is apparent. In an earlier work[14] I argued that it is more fruitful to examine the correlation between these two matters. To do so I must inflict upon the reader a very simple graph. On the *x*-axis we may plot the scale from asymmetric logic to symmetric. On the *y*-axis we may plot the depth of unconscious influence in any particular mental state – remembering of course that this is very much an intuitive matter and not yet accessible to exact measurement. In each case I shall use quite arbitrarily ten units so as to be able to refer simply to different areas of the graph. (See Figure 3.1.)

At the origin, the point (0,0) – where the axes meet we find entirely asymmetric common sense reasoning and no unconscious influence. Mental states at this point are characterised by an absence of emotion and by pure rationality – the state of mind perhaps of a computer, or rather of the human mind when it is most like a computer.

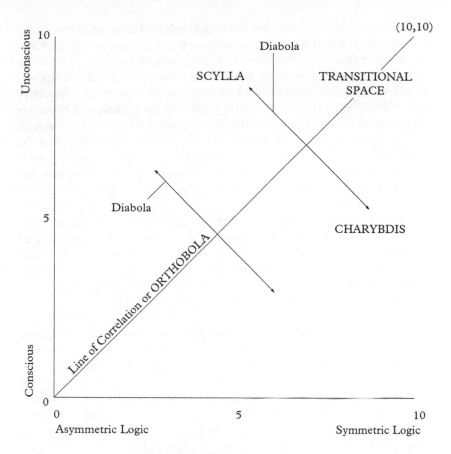

Figure 3.1 Correlation Graph

In total contrast consider now the point (10,10). Here there is no normal reasoning and also symmetric logic is supreme. Every thought has present with it its contradiction or reflection. This is a point further from 'common sense' even than a dream. Matte Blanco linked it with the beatific vision or the goal of the mystic, a state in which there is no awareness of any particular thing or thought and where paradox and eternity meet.

Let us look now at another corner of the graph. (0,10) represents absolute unconsciousness combined with total rationality. None of the paradigmatic instances of unconscious influence – the lover, the madman or the poet[15] – nor dreams, jokes or slips of tongue remotely correspond to this and it would seem that this is empty territory. It represents no mental state that is ever experienced.

The remaining corner is (10,0): totally symmetric logic with total consciousness. Total symmetry means that nothing can be distinguished from anything else, everything is registered as 'the same'. To combine this with total consciousness seems an absurdity, and we may assume this corner is also in empty territory.

If Matte Blanco's theory that symmetry and unconscious influence exactly correspond then all mental states would lie on the line that joins the origin to the point (10,10), the line of correlation between x and y axes. It seems already that there is some degree of correlation for the two points which would most contradict that view are in empty territory. As I have argued already the paranoid state proves that this correlation is not total for in it there is great unconsciousness, and much symmetry, but also some very definite fixed asymmetry. We might place it therefore at, say, (6,9) – the exact figures 6 and 9, as I cautioned, being arbitrarily chosen for purposes of illustration. Richard Carvalho[16] suggests that this is the area corresponding to frozen psychotic states – the mind is frozen into one fixed state. All kinds of obsession correspond to the territory 'above' the line of correlation, for in these mental life is dominated by one specific thought (asymmetry) arising from the unconscious.

On the opposite side of the line of correlation to the paranoid position is the point (9,6). This represents a high but not total degree of unconsciousness and an almost total absence of rational logic – very high symmetry. Carvalho suggests that this corresponds to chaotic psychosis, in which state the mind is incapable of fixing on any defined (asymmetric) thought, although there is some considerable degree of consciousness of the thinking process. Below the line of correlation also belongs the mental illness traditionally called hysteria. The patient is aware to some degree of his or her thinking, but that thinking flies erratically from extreme to extreme without any semblance of logical control. This therefore combines a considerable degree of consciousness with high symmetry.

I shall borrow from classical mythology the terms Scylla and Charybdis to describe the regions respectively above and below the line of correlation. Jason's Argo had to steer between the clashing rocks of Scylla and the swirling whirlpool of Charybdis. Mental states in which the unconscious is stuck asymmetrically upon a fixed thought correspond to shipwreck upon Scylla. Mental states in which consciousness swirls around with the chaos more typical of the symmetry of the Unconscious correspond to entrapment in Charybdis.

There is some evidence that in mental illnesses there can be an alternation between frozen and chaotic psychosis, a sudden transition in terms of the graph from (9,6) to (6,9). The mind is tossed between Scylla and Charybdis and unable to find the channel between. This transition might be represented by a line joining these two points and thus at right angles to the line of correlation. In something of a parallel way there is an oscillation in some mental illness between depression and mania. Depression has a Scylla quality – dominance by the fixed certainty of, say, worthlessness. Mania, on the other hand, swirls chaotically and furiously from one thing to another, consciousness dominated by symmetry. Again, this transition may be represented by a line crossing the line of correlation at right angles. To celebrate resonances which will gradually arise in this discussion I shall call such a line a Diabola, a word of Greek derivation which connotes being 'thrown across' – it is thrown across the line of correlation. The line of correlation I shall call the Orthobola, a word which connotes being 'thrown straight'. The Diabola suggests the diabolic: the Orthobola hints at such religious goals as orthodoxy and orthopraxis, literally right thinking and right doing.

In psychoanalytic theory emotion is seen as rooted in the Unconscious. An emotional state therefore is under some degree of unconscious influence. It is also in emotional states, as has already been argued, that symmetric logic is found even in the sanest mind. Emotional states may therefore be represented by points on or near to the Orthobola if in them there is a correlation between unconscious influence and symmetric logic. A characteristic of sanity, I propose, is that its emotions are accompanied by a corresponding measure of symmetry.

To summarise then what the graph depicts. At the origin: unemotional rationality. On moving up the Orthobola: increasing emotion and growing unconscious influence accompanied by increasing use of symmetric logic. Well to one side – above – the Orthobola we find Scylla, and well to the other – below it – Charybdis. Finally, as we reach the end of the Orthobola we enter the territory of the deepest Unconscious, the goal of the mystic. Way up the Orthobola may be placed the dreamer, though dreams may also stray from the line: not far from the dreamer may be found the lover and the poet, for these three, as Shakespeare declared, are 'of imagination all compact'.

Of particular interest is the area where the Unconscious breaks into consciousness for it is from this area that any direct knowledge of the Unconscious must be obtained. I shall call this area 'transitional space'[17] and the section of the Orthobola which lies in it – we might say from (9,9) to (5,5) – will be the primary focus of our attention, for I shall be arguing that here we encounter not only dreams, declarations of love, and lyric poetry, but also the great myths of humankind. It is in this region that the Unconscious emerges into Consciousness and it is also from this region that conscious material submerges into the Unconscious. This region of the graph represents experiences of profound and powerful emotion, of great beauty, sheer terror, consuming rage, overwhelming love, for in these feelings primary process becomes conscious. Conversely, through events which evoke these feelings conscious experience may become embedded in the Unconscious.

The great stories of humankind have a particular place in subsequent discussion. In so far as they stir deep imaginative feeling, they are working on unconscious levels of the mind, as well as conscious. To do this their logic has to be, in considerable degree, symmetric logic. We turn in the next chapter to a discussion of how this can be.

4   The Modalities of Language

With the concepts derived from Matte Blanco we now need to return briefly to Freud to see how some of the fundamentals of his metapsychology may be expressed anew. In particular the five characteristics of the Unconscious can be shown to arise as consequences of the logic of the Unconscious. That demonstration thereby illustrates their coherence, since all are expressions of symmetric logic. It also suggests a reformulation of them. Each has certain ways of revealing its presence in language, as we have already seen in the case of eternity in Chapter 1, and I shall call these effects the corresponding 'modalities' of language.

Eternity – The First Modality

Matte Blanco noted[1] that if one event is before another in time, to the Unconscious that first event is also after the second. If we call two such events A and B, by the second law of symmetric logic, *A is before B* implies *B is before A*, and we have the conclusion *A and B are simultaneous*. All time is simultaneously present as we have discussed already in Chapter 1. Symmetric logic immediately provides a wider explanation of why the Unconscious is characterised by eternity.

Again in Chapter 1, 'everlastingness' was described as a penultimate form of eternity, eternity expressed within time. The movement from eternity towards temporality is a movement out of the Unconscious towards Consciousness and at the same time the logic we encounter in the expression of this movement begins to admit asymmetry. In the terms of the last chapter, this is a movement 'down the Orthobola' – from point (10,10) to (9,9), and so on. Penultimate forms of eternity are appropriate to transitional space.

The reader may probably agree that it is time to put some empirical flesh on these theoretical bones. Language[2] provides the most accessible and convenient data, for us as it did for Freud. The most primitive and perhaps deepest expression of the eternity of the Unconscious that could be imagined is an unchanging cry of joy or scream of pain, something everlastingly the same. Such would express the dominance of a single extreme emotion pouring out in its most raw form from its unconscious root. The well-known picture by Edvard Munch entitled *The Scream* may serve as an icon of a state of this kind.

More commonly encountered is the occurrence of repetition. Freud observed this in the speech of his patients and connected it with the characteristic of timelessness. Repetition expresses eternity by everlastingly returning to the same point. Anyone who has dealt with people in a state of depression will be familiar with this. Such a patient typically repeats the same words again and again, words expressive of a sense of everlasting defeat or failure. But athletes and footballers in their moments of victory are also given to repetition: 'We did it, we did it' and similar words are used again and again. Repetition seems to do justice to the inner sense of triumph. Likewise, religious feeling is expressed when the church echoes the angels in Isaiah's vision, by saying or singing at every Eucharist, *Holy, Holy, Holy* is the Lord of hosts.[3]

The simplest form of repetition is the use of the same words again and again. Sometimes a person who is emotionally stuck will make the same point repeatedly, but in different words. He or she seems to be groping for something unchanging that no one set of words will adequately express: it could be described as revolving round and round a central point. This is an image of everlasting duration and again may be seen as a reflection of an eternal sameness. I shall refer to this as *repetition with variation*.

Another, more complex and more interesting form of utterance in which symmetry can be discerned is the literary device of *antithetic parallelism*: a statement is made and then repeated with the terms in reverse order. It is not, however, confined to literary contrivance. I heard a radio interview with a young offender who was expressing the powerful feelings brought home to him as his court case reached its climax. He said:

I was about to lose my liberty,
My freedom was about to go.

This is repetition with variation, but the repetition is characterised by a reversal of order, 'my liberty' concluding the first statement and the corresponding term 'my freedom' beginning the second. The beginning and the end are interchanged. The richest source of such antithetic parallelism familiar to the English-speaking reader is the book of Psalms in the *Book of Common Prayer*. For example:

O God, thou knowest my folly:
the wrongs I have done are not hidden from thee.[4]

'God' and 'folly' (= 'wrongs') change places. Similarly, a few verses later:

I am the talk of those who sit in the gate,
and the drunkards make songs about me.[5]

'I' and 'those who talk' (specified in the second line as 'drunkards') again change places. The repetition in this case is less exact since it is not clear whether those who sit in the gate are the same group as the drunkards or not. But their emotive significance to the writer is surely the same – both are speaking of him in similarly disparaging terms.

A compact combination of repetition and antithetic parallelism is found in the words of Jesus in which symmetric logic virtually comes out in the open:

The last will be first,
and the first last.[6]

The three forms of utterance I have so far discussed, repetition, the unchanging cry and antithetic parallelism, are representations of an inner eternity. In *The Four Quartets* T.S. Eliot muses upon how words may express an eternity which he would have seen in religious rather than psychological terms:

Words, after speech, reach
Into the silence. Only by the form, the pattern,
Can words or music reach
The stillness, as a Chinese jar still
Moves perpetually in its stillness,
Not the stillness of the violin, while the note lasts.
Not that only, but the co-existence,
Or say that the end precedes the beginning,
And the end and the beginning were always there
Before the beginning and after the end.
And all is always now.[7]

'The stillness' is the stillness of the eternal, that in which 'all is always now'. This, words can reach, 'only by the form, the pattern'. The 'stillness of the violin, while the note lasts' shares something with an unchanging cry, and though Eliot first seems to deny that it expresses eternal stillness as fully as the Chinese jar, yet his 'Not that only' shows that it does, though not totally. A reversal of beginning and end is needed to make the expression of eternity more complete: the combination of two penultimate forms together more strongly points to the ultimate.

This reversal of end and beginning is taken further in chiasmus which is a wider form of antithetic parallelism. In his *Modern English Usage*[8] Fowler defines it as 'when the terms in the second of two parallel phrases reverse the order of those in the first to which they correspond' and exemplifies it with:

> I cannot dig
> To beg I am ashamed.

The second term does not, as in antithetic parallelism, repeat the meaning of the first, but nevertheless parallells it in a more general way, by addition (as here) or in other instances by contrast. The reversal of order suggests a reversal of time, which of course violates the nature of time and so suggests timelessness. Thereby, as in repetition and antithetic parallelism, the emotion which comes from the speaker's Unconscious is communicated to the Unconscious of the hearer and stirs a similar emotion. (Of course, knowledge of these literary devices enables the speaker to imitate the effects of emotion and thereby communicate something not actually felt – which is doubtless why they are sometimes known as *rhetorical* figures of speech.)

To conclude this point, the language of strong emotion, the language of transitional space as the Unconscious unfolds into Consciousness, expresses eternity in these various penultimate and ante-penultimate ways, through such figures of speech as have been described. The expression of eternity comprises a modality of language, and for the sake of clarity I shall use this word 'modality' as a technical term to refer to such expressions of the Unconscious.

Placelessness – The Second Modality

In the same way that symmetric logic produces timelessness, it also produces placelessness. If A is to the left of B, then B is to the left of A, or above, below, beyond, and so on. Space, like time, is made meaningless. All place is contracted to a single point, or, equally, extended to infinity. One effect of this placelessness is familiar in dreams where one may find oneself simultaneously in several places at once. This is not one of Freud's five characteristics as such, but may be seen as claiming a place beside them and I shall call it *the modality of infinity*.

Just as eternity seen from within time becomes everlastingness (all of time), placelessness or infinity seen from a perspective within space becomes ubiquity or omnipresence (all of space). Just as the very old suggests the everlasting, so the very large suggests the infinite. Just as the very new is timeless (for it has almost no duration), so the infinitesimal too suggests infinity (for it has almost no extension). This relates to the sense of wonder often felt by one first looking through a microscope at the infinitesimal – or through a telescope at the near-infinite distances of space.

Before discussing verbal expressions of infinity it is worth noting that the category of 'emotive speech' may be extended to include written speech. An emotive utterance is generally emotive both to the speaker and to the hearer – to communicate emotion is usually its purpose. Those same forms of speech, such as repetition, which express emotion in the speaker, also typically induce emotion in the hearer. Those features which express the Unconscious of one will speak to the Unconscious of another – not, of course, infallibly, but, one might say, when the communication is successful. For this reason what is written with the intention of speaking to the Unconscious will have the same features as what is spontaneously spoken under unconscious influence. Thus just as an ingenious actor may mimic emotive speech without emotion, so an ingenious writer may mimic emotive speech without emotion, so as to induce emotion in the reader. This ingenuity constitutes the art of rhetoric, which is among other things the conscious imitation of the forms of speech which unconscious influence imposes. In this sense the art of rhetoric is not the preserve of the public orator alone, but, for example, also of the poet. We see here the germ of a theory of how poetry achieves its effects.

A compendium of the forms of rhetorical speech may be found in Fowler's *Modern English Usage*.[9] Almost all the 'tropes' or 'figures of speech' which he lists may be seen as expressions of symmetric logic. Chiasmus is an instance both of the modality of eternity (when spoken), and of infinity (in written form). In general this will be true of the other phenomena, such as repetition, discussed above: what takes time to express in spoken form, takes space literally upon the page. The reversal of time becomes a reversal of space. Chiasmus, it may be noted, derives its name from the written form since it comes from the Greek letter chi, which looks much like a capital X.

There are other figures of speech which fall under both modalities. For example, climax (meaning 'ladder') is 'the arrangement of a series of notions in such an order that each is more impressive than the preceding'.[10] Fowler quotes:

Eye hath not seen, nor ear heard, neither have entered into the heart of man the things which God hath prepared.

The ladder carries the hearer upward and an infinite extension is suggested, as when an infinite numerical series is designated by its first terms (e.g., 1,4,9, etc. – the beginning of the series of square numbers). There is a device recognised in mediaeval rhetoric in which the ascending notions are of increasing length. For example, from the Church of England's *Alternative Service Book*:

Holy Father, heavenly King, almighty and eternal God.[11]

Form walks hand in hand with meaning and thus the ascent towards infinity is underlined.

Symbolism – The Third Modality

Freud's Displacement and Condensation are situations in which the Unconscious, blind to distinctions, identifies things with a certain similarity and transfers attributes of one thing to another. Matte Blanco's symmetrisation may be seen as generalising these two characteristics. Anything may be identified with any class to which it belongs. That class may then be represented in Consciousness by any other member of it and matters appropriate to the first member transferred to the second. I propose to call the linguistic expressions of this category *symbolism*, though not in the technical psychoanalytic sense.[12] By symbolism I mean any expression of this characteristic of exchanging one thing for another and attaching to the second feelings and thoughts that belong to the first. This comes about by means of a symmetrisation through which both things are replaced in the Unconscious by a common class. Symbolism, after eternity and infinity, is the third modality of the Unconscious.

The primary linguistic expression of symbolism is *metaphor*, a figure of speech easy to recognise, very hard to define. Janet Soskice, in *Metaphor and Religious Language*,[13] devotes many pages to discussion of such definitions and in establishing her own:

Metaphor is that figure of speech whereby we speak about one thing in terms which are seen to be suggestive of another.

Traditional theories of metaphor, she argues, are apt to be based on a limited range consisting of those metaphors in which one term replaces another: 'Man is a wolf', for example. It is customary and natural to understand such as a comparison between the two terms. But many metaphors, Soskice argues, are not like this: 'writhing script' is not necessarily a comparison between some writing and a snake, or any other specific creature that 'writhing' may bring to mind. Different hearers may conjure up different images, for many things can writhe, people in pain as well as snakes, and no particular image has a claim to primacy.

In terms of the present discussion, what a metaphor achieves is to invite the hearer to consider a term as one of a set with which it perhaps might not otherwise be classified, and then to draw characteristics from other members of that set. Thus if some writing is described as 'writhing script' it is being assigned to the genus of writhing objects. Attributes of other members of the genus may then be applied to the script. One member of the genus thus potentially inherits the attributes of all. So far, these are just suggested, hanging in the air as it were. Some of them may then be spelt out, by extending the metaphor. The writhing script may 'terminate in an agony of pain'. Or it may 'gradually fade away, sliding into its burrow'. Whether the metaphor is actually extended by the speaker or not, a range of suggestions is invoked (by a living and successful metaphor) and feeling drawn from more than one source may be experienced in the context to which the metaphor refers.

Another metaphor Soskice discusses at length is drawn from the poetry of e.e. cummings:[14]

nobody, not even the rain, has such small hands.

The metaphor casts up in the reader's mind:

thoughts of what kind of hands rain might have, suggestions of fragility, delicacy, transience, ability to reach the smallest places.

She adds:

The purpose of the metaphor is both to cast up and organise a network of associations.

This network of associations is drawn from a range of sources and the purpose of the metaphor is to relate the referent of the metaphor to these sources. The relation thus established invites the hearer to displace the associations from source to referent. In the case of a dead metaphor this displacing does not normally happen because conventional use has so familiarised the link that it is no longer sensed as a link – a metaphor – at all. This then becomes an instance

where the language shows a symmetry which does not proceed from
or induce unconscious feeling.

It may be objected that even a living metaphor does not induce in
the hearer displacement and condensation in their proper Freudian
meaning. In a true example of condensation, such as is found in a
dream, the dreamer experiences source and referent as one and the
same. There is no awareness that they are in reality separate. In most
uses of metaphor this is not so. If we say 'Man is a wolf', we are
aware that man is not literally a wolf. Asymmetric distinction here
lives alongside symmetric identification. Therefore, we see, as with
eternity, a scale from the strongest to the weaker forms of expression.
For example, a patient who howled like a wolf would be expressing
more of the Unconscious than one who repeatedly stated metaphor-
ically, 'I am a wolf.' And that in turn would be stronger than the
corresponding simile, 'I am like a wolf.' Expressions of identity,
metaphor, and simile constitute a descending scale of both unconscious process and of symmetric logic. These may again be described
as ultimate, penultimate and ante-penultimate forms of a modality.

Non-contradiction – The Fourth Modality

The non-contradiction of opposite drives in the Unconscious which
Freud noted takes a logical form in Matte Blanco's thinking. Assertions
are accompanied by their opposites and both are entertained at once.
The verbal expression of total contradiction is simply contradiction.
But in less total, less symmetric, more conscious form we find also
paradox, in which the contradiction may be mainly apparent, and
antinomy in which there is generally only a show of contradiction.

There are three other interesting figures of speech which may be
seen as expressions of non-contradiction, sometimes in combination
with the expression of other characteristics.

Aposiopesis is the device of falling silent, breaking off unexpectedly
in the middle of speech. Fowler's instance is: If we should fail –.
Boundless possibilities of disaster are suggested, more varied and all-
encompassing than any specific statement. There is a paradoxical
equivalence between nothing and everything, which relates to other
situations, especially in theology, where nothing and everything have
more in common than either has with any one specific thing. God,
the ineffable about whom strictly nothing can be said, is everything
or nothing, but never a finite specific thing. Again, mathematically,
zero and infinity are reciprocals in so far as either has a reciprocal.
This trope thus relates to two of the principal manifestations of
symmetry – infinity and paradox.

In *hyperbole* exaggerated terms are used, not for deception, but for emphasis. Fowler refers to the use of 'infinite' for 'great', and 'a thousand apologies' for an apology. The use of an absurdly large round number, like the word 'infinite' itself, is a rather obvious way of heightening significance by importing infinity to express emotion. A more interesting figure of speech is hyperbole's opposite, *meiosis*, understatement which has something in common with aposiopesis. To call something 'good', 'excellent' or 'superb' is to specify just where it stands on some intuitive scale of merit: to call it 'not bad' in some uses is more powerful because it points the hearer to goodness of no specified degree, and therefore potentially to goodness of an unlimited degree – and again the infinite may be evoked. This example of meiosis is an instance also of litotes, in which, for a positive notion, the negation of a negative is used. There is a suggestion of paradox implicit in this, whereby the notion it is desired to communicate is best expressed through its opposite. Not strictly litotes, yet related, is the current youth slang where 'wicked' means 'very good'. Or a usage recently heard from a young speaker at a farewell presentation:

> She's bad. [Pause, in which the speaker became aware that the audience was partly adult and possibly therefore uncomprehending.] I don't mean bad, really bad, but bad really good.[15]

This is litotes without the second negation but the effect is similar, as is the implicit symmetry. Both this and litotes proper relate to the manifestation of the absence of contradiction. The opposite notion is raised and even where it is negated a shadow of this opposite remains, for in some popular speech a double negative is not self-cancelling, but intensifying ('I ain't never going to do that') as it is in French (*ne ... pas*, are both in themselves negatives).

It is however in *oxymoron* that this manifestation comes wholly into its own. The word itself means 'sharp-dull': its characteristic is that directly opposite terms are used together in defiance of natural meaning. It is thus among epithets what a paradox is among statements, another highly symmetrical way of expressing or inducing unconscious weight. As Fowler puts it, its 'exceptional coincidence is therefore arresting'.[16] As in previous instances, a manifestation of symmetric logic, of apparent nonsense, catches hold of the hearer, a phenomenon which my argument attributes to its impact on unconscious levels of the mind. Christian theology is particular addicted to oxymoron: true God and true man, a just man and a sinner both at once, and most compact of all, 'the Virgin Mother'.

I shall postpone discussion for the moment of Freud's fifth characteristic, the equivalence of fantasy and reality. The first four revised

and generalised by Matte Blanco's symmetric logic give us four types
of verbal expression of unconscious process: Expressions of eternity,
expressions of infinity, symbolism and paradox. The power to
express and to move is found most powerfully when these different
manifestations of symmetry work together in combination. Then the
symmetry is disguised. A complex interweaving of symmetries
presents an opacity which itself expresses the Unconscious, whereas
the artifice of a simple expression may be too apparent to
Consciousness. I shall illustrate this shortly, but first some other
devices must be discussed.

Alliteration is a device by which the linking of the sound of words
links their meaning too. It achieves this by the *repetition* of the sound
of the initial letter or letters. The alliterative words thereby become
repetition with variation of each other. A standing still is achieved by
which the meaning of the separate words is compacted together into
a single new meaning. This compacting together, of the many
becoming one, is reminiscent of symbolism. *Assonance* is a similar
phenomenon in which sounds, usually vowel sounds, are deliberately
repeated, the echo achieving its effect for the same reason as does
alliteration, by the compacting together of many into one.

Related to these is *paronomasia*, better known as *punning*. Fowler
describes it as 'making jocular or suggestive use of similarity between
different words or of a word's different senses'. [17]While taking due
note of Freud's attention to jokes, we will need to distinguish sharply
between the jocular and the suggestive. It is the former use which has
given punning a bad name: the clumsy pun is a conversation stopper
to all but those with very simple taste in humour. The more suggestive pun, by contrast, is of pivotal importance in poetry, most strikingly perhaps in that of Shakespeare. A word appears with its
expected meaning, but its other meanings carry unexpected
emotional resonances, and these are compounded together in a way
that shares something with metaphor. The single word evokes many
meanings and this appearance of the many in the one is another
instance of the modality of symbolism.

Alliteration, assonance and paronomasia use sound to reinforce
sense and thereby achieve a simultaneous discharge of multiple
meaning into one, an identity of class and member. Together with
unexpected reversals and repetitions, and the use of metaphor, these
are of the essence of most poetry. The American poet Robert Frost
wrote:

My poems – I should suppose everybody's poems – are all set to
trip the reader head foremost into the boundless.[18]

What can he mean by 'the boundless' if not the Unconscious, the infinite, the eternal? The rhetorical devices are a principal means of this tripping, and the reason they trip is because they express the symmetric logic of the Unconscious, primarily through the four avenues I have so far described.

I have already suggested that in poetic speech, effects are achieved very generally; not by a single use of a rhetorical device, but by their combination. Consider so simple an instance as Job's reflection:

> The Lord has given,
> The Lord has taken away.
> Blessed be the Name of the Lord.[19]

There is anaphora (marked repetition of a phrase) in the double use of 'The Lord has ...' Much weaker would be the substitute, 'The Lord has given and taken away'. The two first lines are in parallel, yet their meaning is opposite. Together they form something close to an oxymoron. The two issue in an exclamation of praise of God. The exclamation thus interpreted might be rewritten:

> Blessed be the God of symmetry.

Far more complex instances of the weaving of figures of speech may readily be found. Consider these lines of Shakespeare, for example:

> *Methought I heard a voice cry, 'Sleep no more!*
> *Macbeth does murder sleep', the innocent sleep,*
> *Sleep that knits up the ravelled sleave of care,*
> *The death of each day's life, sore labour's bath,*
> *Balm of hurt minds, great nature's second course,*
> *Chief nourisher in life's feast.*[20]

There are eight metaphors: 'knits up', 'ravelled sleave', 'death', 'bath', 'balm', 'course', 'nourisher' and 'feast', not including those in the second line, which are instances of another trope, metonomy (the use of an attribute of something to stand for it): for sleep is an attribute of the sleeping Duncan. But the word is also acting as a pivot for the transition from the murder to a general encomium of sleep, and this pivoting has the nature of a pun, for the listener will hear both the ordinary meaning of 'sleep' and its special meaning as a metonomy for Duncan. In the last line there is an asyndeton, a trope in which phrases are compacted together by the omission of conjunctions. The compacting effect of asyndeton is reinforced by the alliteration which also joins these phrases to each other, 'sleep' to 'sleave', 'life' to 'labour's', 'bath' to 'balm', 'care' leaping over to 'course' and a kind of evolving alliteration in the last line, 'ch' to 'sh' to the s's in 'life's feast', with its two f's as well.

The 'trip into the boundless' that Frost spoke of is inconceivable without these figures of speech, tropes or rhetorical devices. They are of the essence of the artifice of poetry. Whether in the hands of a master poet or as the unthinking expression of genuine feeling they are essential to emotive communication and in every case to greater or less degree either their content or their form or both is an expression of symmetric logic.

Fantasy and Reality – The Fifth Modality

Freud's fifth characteristic of the Unconscious is its inability to distinguish fantasy and reality. This may be seen as a particular case of the working together of other characteristics, since if a story is lodged in the Unconscious, the Unconscious cannot regard it as true, without also regarding it as false. If it seems to take place in one specific time and place, it will at once become timeless and placeless. Thus the story or memory of an event in the Unconscious cannot be distinguished from fantasy.

If, therefore, a story expresses unconscious content or engages with it to some degree, it is in that same degree beyond the distinction between reality and fantasy. This accounts for the power of story-telling – the hearer can be transported into a world of make-believe, and during the telling the make-believe has a degree of reality. This is particularly so where the hearer, or reader, identifies strongly with a hero or heroine of the story – identification is an instance of the third modality. There are stories which have little of this property and an uncrafted record of mere facts may retain a sense of straightforward reality. The gifted novelist, by contrast, is likely to make much use of the third modality. The proffer of identification is perhaps most typical of the great Victorian novels – *David Copperfield* or *Jane Eyre*, for example. Other symbolisms are possible: for example, trivial incidents may be recounted in ways which make them suggestive of greater events to come and in this way a sense of coherent pattern may be communicated. The same effect, much used by Shakespeare, is the telling of a sub-plot which partially echoes the main story, as Gloucester's misfortunes echo Lear's. Sub-plots may echo in reverse to the same effect, as Banquo's story does Macbeth's. Such use of the modality of symbolism expresses the writer's Unconscious and engages with that of the reader. The more overt, and therefore conscious, the use of such devices is, the less it is likely to be effective. This accounts for the weakness of allegory, a story in which a point for point translation into fact may be made: and for the power of great stories where the relationship to reality is veiled in ambiguities. What, for example, does the albatross represent in Coleridge's *The Ancient Mariner*, or the Holy Grail in the Arthurian cycle? In Chapter 7 this important modality will be discussed in connection with fairy stories and with myths.

Table 1.1 on page 15 showed a tabulation of the various expressions of timelessness. We may now similarly tabulate all five modalities (Table 4.1).

Table 4.1 Summary of the Modalities

Timelessness	Placelessness	Part-for-Whole	Non-Contradiction	Non-reality
		Ultimate forms		
Eternity	Infinity	Total Identity of part and whole	Co-presence of opposites	No distinction between truth and fantasy
		Penultimate forms		
Everlasting	Infinite extension	Part treated as whole	Irreconcilable paradox	Fantasy treated as truth and Truth treated as fantasy
Momentary	Infinitesimal	Whole treated as part		
		Ante-penultimate forms		
The Ancient	The Immense	Symbols	Apparent paradox	Story – the suspension of disbelief
The New	The Minute			

Conclusion

I will now summarise what this chapter has provided. The theory that the Unconscious is profoundly symmetrical and operates by the laws of symmetric logic enables us to describe and understand the language of emotion. The empirical evidence summarised in Freud's five characteristics can be reformulated as expressions of the Unconscious in five principal modalities. These have been discussed primarily in terms of language. They will be found in dreams, in lyric poetry, in liturgical language and in the spontaneous expressions of profound emotion. Each may take a hierarchy of forms, ultimate, penultimate and ante-penultimate of decreasing degrees of symmetry. The strongest forms will generally be found in expressions most influenced by unconscious process. They will thus be the currency especially of transitional space. The weaker forms will penetrate far down the Orthobola into conscious process where common-sense logic is prevalent.

5   God and the Unconscious

In this chapter it is argued that the God which the mystics seek in the depths of the soul is to be identified with the depths of the Unconscious. This provides a starting point for any description of what the word 'God' means. Yet Christian faith has other, more specific, things to say of God. It is therefore proposed that the mystics' God be called 'The Unconscious of God' and that any other aspect of God be attributed to 'The Consciousness of God'.

It is now possible to discuss the nature of God by means of the metapsychological concepts described in earlier chapters. I address first the nature of the God of the mystics.

Jacob or Israel the father of the nation lay down to sleep and while he slept he dreamed:

> He [Jacob] came to a certain shrine and, because the sun had gone, he stopped for the night. He took one of the stones there and, using it as a pillow under his head, he lay down to sleep. In a dream he saw a ladder, which rested on the ground with its top reaching to heaven, and angels of God were going up and down on it. The Lord was standing beside him saying, 'I am the Lord, the God of your father Abraham and the God of Isaac'.[1]

The fourteenth-century author of *The Seven Steps of the Ladder of Spiritual Love*[2] is by no means alone in using Jacob's Ladder as a symbol of his mystical journey. The dream is marked, as dreams are, by at least two of the modalities described in previous chapters: infinity, or placelessness, since God is both, one assumes, at the top of the ladder and also standing beside Jacob – and symbolism in the image of the ladder itself. I shall now explore the proposal that the mystical ascent is also a descent into the Unconscious.

Many witnesses might be called to support this proposal. I appeal to William Johnston, a Jesuit expert in Western mysticism but a student also of Buddhism, who has written, among other books, a general introduction to mysticism entitled *The Inner Eye of Love*.[3] Johnston is arguing for a degree of rapprochement between Christian

and Buddhist approaches and displays no special interest in psychoanalytic matters. He might therefore be counted as a disinterested
witness for my purpose. Nevertheless, he finds it necessary to refer to
modern psychology. For example, he writes:

> But there is a human question which psychology never asks and
> which leads people to religion; namely, what is at the deepest
> realm of the psyche? What is the basis or centre or root of all? Put
> in Jungian terms I might ask: When I go beyond the ego, beyond
> the personal unconscious, beyond the collective unconscious,
> beyond the archetypes, what do I find? And in answer to this all
> the great religions speak of a mystery which they call by various
> names: the Buddha nature, Brahman and Atman, the divine spark,
> the ground of being, the centre of the soul, the kingdom of God,
> the image of God and so on. They use different terms; But all, I
> believe, are pointing towards a single reality.[4]

Johnston argues that at this deep level of psychic life there is found the
presence of God, a fullness and an all-encompassing love. In particular he concludes from a discussion of St John of the Cross that:

> Mysticism opens up a new layer of psychic life which is bitter and
> unpleasant because of its unfamiliarity. But when the eye of love
> becomes accustomed to the dark, it perceives that the darkness is
> light and the void is plenitude.[5]

Johnston is not entirely happy with the word 'unconscious'. He
roundly asserts that 'nothing is unconscious in the psyche'.[6]
Nevertheless, for him the mystic is clearly travelling into territory that
psychology calls the Unconscious.

> This psychology speaks in terms of state or layers of consciousness
> rather than faculties of the soul. In the mystical life one passes
> from one layer to the next in an inner or downward journey to the
> core of the personality where dwells the great mystery called God
> – God who cannot be known directly, cannot be seen (for no man
> has ever seen God) and who dwells in thick darkness. This is the
> never-ending journey which is recognisable in the mysticism of all
> the great religions.[7]

We may conclude that for Johnston the mystical journey is made by
the conscious mind into territory that otherwise is unconscious. If he
asserts that no part of the mind is wholly unconscious, it is because the
enterprise he describes is the making of the Unconscious conscious.

Through the mystical journey 'the consciousness gradually expands and integrates data from the so-called unconscious while the whole personality is absorbed into the great mystery of God'.[8]

For Johnston the mystical journey is not an esoteric pursuit for the few. It is open to all as an element in every human life. He believes that there is a universal call to contemplation and he quotes Karl Rahner to the effect that mystical experience is 'not different from the ordinary life of grace'.[9] Mysticism is the core of authentic religious experience and is for everyone, not 'just for all Christians but for all men'.

Some writers dispute this belief in a universal call. Among such is the fourteenth-century anonymous author of *The Cloud of Unknowing*.[10] He believed that only a few were called to the mystical journey, because it is difficult and dangerous. This danger does not arise from strange and esoteric phenomena, which are peripheral to the mystical enterprise, though much favoured by mystical quackery. For the author of *The Cloud*, the danger comes from self-deception and from the Devil's desire to thwart anyone who wants union with God.

Yet for the author of *The Cloud*, as for Johnston, the mystical path, though a special calling, is concerned with universal human realities: it is an exploration in this life of the bliss that shall last for ever in heaven.[11] While it is the call of only a few to pursue it in this life, it is the path which, in the end, the redeemed will all pursue. The mystic begins his journey by offering himself to God, 'lapping and clothing the feeling of God in the feeling of himself'.[12] He is seeking God through his own soul. The work of the mystic is to put aside every thought and feeling of any particular thing and to cover all such with a cloud of forgetting. He then directs his will with a naked love and nothing else towards God. Before him there is a cloud of unknowing, a darkness without shape or form beyond or within which is God. 'And well is this work likened to a sleep'[13] since the mind is to be entirely stilled. All thought of anything is to be trodden down and held under 'a cloud of forgetting'.[14]

While the language of metapsychology was of course unknown to the author of *The Cloud* we can recognise that he is describing this same descent into zones of the mind that today would be called unconscious. In discussing such inherently slippery concepts as the Unconscious and the God of the mystics, to seek for certain proof would be absurd. I propose, however, that the similarities of language are very strong and rather than multiplying such witnesses I will leap forthwith to the conclusion that the God of the mystics is encountered in the depths of what psychoanalysis terms the Unconscious. The mystical journey is an attempt by the conscious mind to enter the realm that otherwise is wholly unconscious.

It is superficially a strange thing that psychoanalysts talk of individual consciousness but generally of *the* Unconscious. It is as though, even for the hard-headed practitioner with no metaphysical interests, the depth of the Unconscious is single, not possessed uniquely by the individual. Jung, particularly, wrote of a transition from the individual to the collective Unconscious, as though greater depth led to greater unity. Similarly, no mystic writes of reaching a private God, but rather of penetration to something that is the one eternal all and no-thing.

I shall therefore describe that which the mystic glimpses as, not just his or her Unconscious, but the Unconscious of God, an Unconscious at its deepest level shared by every animate being. Some may consider this deepest level to be indeed just nothingness. By calling this nothingness 'the Unconscious of God' I do not intend to import in an underhand way the notion that there is a being somewhere 'out there' corresponding to the conventional picture of God. What I do intend to suggest is that there is something universal in the kind of experience people have of this deep level; and that this nothingness is also felt to be an experience of 'everything', as well as of 'nothing'. Furthermore I imply that this experience of nothing and everything is what the Christian mystics describe as an experience of God. What sort of God this is, and what content, if any, his being may have, are, at this point, open questions. I say this in the hope of reassuring any reader who does not believe in a 'realist' God that he or she is not being tricked into such a belief by this terminology.

On the other hand, some believers may find it peculiar, or even blasphemous, to talk of 'the Unconscious of God'. Yet if God may be described symbolically as having a finger, a hand, an eye, and indeed a mind, then symbolically also it seems unreasonable to forbid positing an Unconscious and a Consciousness in that mind. More accurately one might speak of something analogous to the Unconscious, and of something analogous to Consciousness. I do not intend to speculate whether, to God, his own Unconscious is open to his Consciousness, nor to suggest that his actions proceed from a region of himself unknown to him. I shall however make use of a distinction in our thoughts of God between those that relate to the analogue in him of the Unconscious and those which relate to the analogue in him of Consciousness: thus the mystic approaches the Unconscious of God, but the God of the Jewish and Christian Scriptures is often very differently described. He is a God whom the prophets call upon to *remember* his afflicted people. He is a God who has very clear preferences and is even capable of apparently wilful behaviour. Jacob he loved, but Esau he hated. Abel's sacrifice he accepted, whereas Cain's he inexplicably rejected, and so on. Such a

God is not adequately described as unconscious only: I shall use the term 'the Consciousness of God' to refer to the aspect of God that such language appears to impute to him.

Whether this distinction is real in God is doubtless unknowable: it is however implicit in the language of the Christian faith about God. The terms I have used for the distinction have been made available primarily by the discoveries of Freud, yet what they express is very similar to what the theology of the Eastern Orthodox church calls 'the Essence' of God and 'the Energies' of God. The essence is utterly unknowable and inconceivable to humanity. It is what God is in himself. The Energies of God are knowable through his disclosure of himself. They are described by one orthodox theologian, John Meyendorff, as follows:

> God does however makes himself known outside of his transcendent nature. 'God is manifested by His "powers" in all beings, is multiplied without abandoning His unity.' Thus, the concepts of beauty, being, goodness, and the like, reflect God, but not His essence, only His 'powers' and 'energies', which are however not a diminished form of deity, or mere emanations, but themselves fully God, in whom created beings can participate in the proportion and analogy proper to each.[15]

Meyendorff quotes the fourth-century theologian Gregory of Nyssa to make a similar point:

> In speaking of God, when there is question of His essence, then is the time to keep silence. When, however it is a question of His operation, a knowledge of which can come down even to us, that is the time to speak of his omnipotence by telling of His works and explaining His deeds, and to use words to this extent.[16]

I quote Meyendorff to suggest that some distinction of the kind that I propose is not a novel one. Another contrast of the greatest interest is made between the essence and the energies. Meyendorff is summarising the thoughts of Pseudo-Dionysus, the fifth-century father of mysticism in both Eastern and Western churches. 'For knowledge can apply only to "beings", and God is above being and superior to all opposition between being and non-being.'[17] Of the essence of God, therefore, it cannot be asserted either that it is or that it is not: it is beyond both being and non-being.

This ambivalence about the very existence of God throws light on an issue touched upon already: the notion that both the Unconscious and the goal of the mystic are not private, but are one and the same in every individual. For if the mystic reaches non-being, that is to say nothingness, then nothingness is simply one and the same. One person's nothingness is presumably the same as another person's. If on the other hand the mystic is experiencing the unity of everything – touching 'everything' , one might say – then again that is one and the same. There cannot be two or more 'everythings'. What seems indisputably common to all accounts of mysticism is that it is not about experiencing something, in the sense of *some thing*.

To argue in that way is, perhaps, simply to play upon words and many will dismiss it as such. Yet mystics in many cultures have expressed their thoughts in words of that kind, and with the greatest earnestness. The alliance of nothing and everything, over against any particular something, has an interesting resonance in elementary mathematics. For every ordinary number has a reciprocal – the result of dividing it into one – except zero. If zero is divided into one, there is no answer except possibly (in a loose and dangerous sense mathematically) infinity, and infinity is not a proper number.

The eternal and infinite One, which is both All and Nothing: language of this kind is apparently foreign to the modern Westerner. It may seem to have little to do with the faith inspired by Jesus Christ, and yet that faith soon became entangled with those who found such language of fundamental significance. From the early Greek philosophers Pythagoras and Parmenides, through Plato and Aristotle to the Neo-Platonists, ultimate reality was apt to be debated in terms of the relationship between the One and the Many – the one ultimate whatever it was, and the many particulars of ordinary experience. The fathers of the Christian church were engaged in this debate, vigorously conducted against philosophical Neo-Platonists and religious Gnostics. To attempt to summarise it here would be impossible, but it is important to remember that the doctrines of the Trinity and Incarnation, as still held today, were hammered out in this context.

A vital point of disagreement between Christians and Neo-Platonists was precisely the relationship of the One to the Many. To the Neo-Platonists the One was an undifferentiated monad without real relationship to the world: to the Christian the One, who was God, was the creator of the world and active in it in pursuit of an eternal loving purpose.

There would be little point in re-visiting this ancient debate here were it not that Matte Blanco's theory of bi-logic offers a new understanding of it – and therefore of the Christian doctrines which emerged from it. It would be an absurd anachronism to claim that the debate was *really* about the Unconscious and Consciousness, for these are modern terms. Yet a debate on remarkably parallel lines emerges from Matte Blanco's theory, and one which may allow us to re-appropriate the language of the doctrines of the Trinity and Incarnation in a metapsychological setting: for Matte Blanco's symmetry reduces the many to the One, whereas his asymmetry is concerned with the discrimination of the many particulars. Therefore the possibility emerges that he has provided a logic that throws light on the ancient debates and upon the paradoxical doctrines that emerged from them. This logic throws a similar light, too, upon the mystical writers and upon the transcendental experiences discussed in Chapter 1. The possibility emerges of finding new connections between these and the traditional language of the Christian faith.

If we look at the writings of the mystics in the light of bi-logic we are immediately struck by the prevalence of symmetric logic. Whatever is asserted has very soon to be denied. With the author of *The Cloud* we are asked to leave aside every specific thought, even specific thoughts of God. If we think such and such of God, we must at once deny it. All specific assertions are overthrown in this way. If we follow that author's mentor, Pseudo-Dionysus, we are to end even in denying that God is, and then at once, that he is not, since he is beyond both being and non-being. We are invited, in fact, to precisely that condition which a total use of symmetric logic brings about, an absolute absence of any specific thought whatever. The law of opposition is ruthlessly to be followed to the end. God is nothing, and God is everything, and God is beyond both everything and nothing, and even one might say beyond neither everything nor nothing. If any assertions are to be made in this region they might, perhaps, be the koans of the Zen Buddhist,[18] assertions so inherently meaningless that they divert the mind from clinging to any meaning whatsoever.

If we return to the graph of Figure 3.1 (p. 39), it is clear that the Unconscious of God corresponds to the point (10,10) – speech about it is ruled wholly by symmetric logic (10 on the x-axis), and, by definition, it is the deepest Unconscious (10 on the y-axis). That is where, we may say, the Neo-Platonists and the Gnostics were content to leave their monad: it was utterly ineffable (nothing could be said of it – total symmetry) and utterly unknowable (the deepest Unconscious). We may now in a very speculative and theoretical way explore how the Christian mystics have amended that simple picture, and with the mystics, the fathers of orthodox Christianity.

Johnston, again in *The Inner Eye of Love*, concludes that the mystics of both East and West have by and large concurred in the experience that a deep sense of unity is bestowed by their journey, an experience that the Christian may well call love. The ultimate One is not after all as neutral as the Neo-Platonists thought it. The deepest

Unconscious, the Unconscious of God, is not a totally neutral nothingness, but bestows on those who approach it a sense of cosmic
unity and universal love.

We may identify three descriptions of the ultimate in terms of bi-
logic:

1. that which is entirely symmetrical, of which nothing may be said
    without being unsaid, the all or nothing beyond being and non-
    being
2. that which is symmetrical in all respects, except that it is, rather
    than is not; even though it may be described as both all and
    nothing
3. that which in addition induces a sense of love (rather than indif-
    ference).

All these positions are very symmetrical, but there is a growth of
asymmetry in the movement from the first to the last.

The language of the mystics has placed God in all three of these
logical positions, and we may call these descriptions of the
Unconscious of God. The language of Christian faith has many other
things to say of God that are not encompassed by these.
Nevertheless, the Unconscious of God is of the greatest importance.
It gives an initial placing of the meaning of the word 'God' to those
for whom talk of God suggests crude images – the old man seated on
the clouds, and so forth. It roots the search for God in the depths of
the human soul, rather than, for example, in the explanation of gaps
in cosmology. It therefore opens communication to many whose
occasional experiences seem to echo some of the thoughts of the
mystics. It provides the beginning of a language to speak of 'transcendental experience'.

Not all transcendental experience is benign and bi-logic throws
some light on the nearness of the divine and the demonic. The third
description, which, according to Johnston, is preferred by both
Buddhist and Christian faiths, might be summarised in the assertion
'There is love.' The writings of the mystics abound in paradox: it is
their chief linguistic characteristic. The modality of paradox was
derived from the first law of symmetric logic: one-term propositions
imply their negations. It might be expected therefore that alongside
'There is love' should be found also 'There is hate.' Yet an argument
can be supported for assigning a greater degree of symmetry to love
than to hate. Love is essentially an experience of unity, in this case a
unity with everything or nothing. On the other hand the notion of
hate seems to imply a distinction between the hater and the hated: in
this case between the would-be mystic and the mystic's goal. Since it

implies a distinction it has an element of asymmetry implicit in it, which love does not.

The possibility of hate, even of total universal hate, requires the distinction between the one who hates and what is hated. Universal hate is therefore expressible in the assertion, '*I hate everything.*' This is not the symmetrical opposite of '*There is love*' but of '*I love everything*': an assertion in which a distinction has also emerged between the lover and the loved. Once the sense of self is present symmetry presents the danger of hate. The author of *The Cloud* warns against having any sense of the self at all:

> Strip, spoil and utterly unclothe thyself of all manner of feeling of thyself, that thou mayest be able to be clothed with the gracious feeling of God himself.[19]

If 'I' is present in the deepest Unconscious, then there is a specific particularity, an asymmetry there, for otherwise symmetry would cancel out 'I' with 'not-I'. If 'I' is present we are therefore not at (10,10), but, at say, (9,10): deepest Unconscious, not with total symmetry, but with some asymmetry too. This point falls in the region of the graph described as Scylla. Since, I have suggested, total universal hate implies a sense of the distinction between self and other, it implies the presence of an 'I', and therefore corresponds to a point in the region of Scylla. The mystic who is in the state describable as '*I love everything*' is risking the symmetric transformation of this into its opposite, into '*I hate everything.*' Perhaps that is why the author of *The Cloud* warns the reader against 'loving everything'. He was aware that having thought or desire directed 'to creatures in general',[20] even though it be a loving thought, is dangerous, since it passes easily into hating creatures in general, an instance of the first law of symmetric logic, the law of opposition.

If we play for a moment with the possibilities suggested by symmetric logic, we may identify other dangers. Awareness of the self will change the sense that '*There is love*', unfolding it asymmetrically into '*I love everything*' as suggested above. Since we are still in dominantly symmetric territory, the law of two-term reflection may draw the symmetric deduction '*Everything loves me.*' To feel oneself loved by God or the All-Nothing may be benign: to believe that every particular being loves one is pathological. It shares something with the state of infantile omnipotence in which everything exists to fulfil one's will. Symmetry is total, since any and every particular is felt as loving – there is no distinction between particulars. But this love is felt, there is a degree of consciousness, and therefore this state corresponds to the point, let us say, (10,9) – total symmetry, some consciousness. This is in the region called Charybdis, the whirlpool. The image is appropriate for the state of manic frenzy which this state suggests: any and every particular thing is the bearer of universal, infinite love and desire. Any particular thing is thus equated with the infinite whole which thereby is treated as finite, as containable by a particular. In short, Charybdis treats the infinite as finite, it attempts to finitise the infinite.

'*I love everything*' symmetrically implies 'I hate everything': and '*Everything loves me*' symmetrically implies '*Everything hates me.*' These possibilities of falling into Scylla or into Charybdis are real dangers and the mystical literature speaks of such. To quote the same passage of *The Cloud* more fully:

> And do that in thee is to forget all the creatures that ever God made and the works of them, so that thy thought or thy desire be not directed or stretched to any of them, neither in general nor in special. But let them be, and take no heed of them ... All fiends be mad when thou dost thus, and try for to defeat it in all that they can.[21]

There is an account of such a fall from grace in Traherne's account of the childhood experience already quoted in Chapter 1 (p. 9). Having seen everything wrapped in a glorious unity, Traherne is so attracted by it that he seeks to grasp it, or some part of it, for his own possession, and he is at once corrupted and 'made to learn the Dirty Devices of this World.' This corruption is covetousness, the desire to hold for private pleasure what is an essentially public and communal good.

Traherne sounds like a child gazing at a beautiful picture in a public gallery, who then wants to cut out and take home for him or her self some specially attractive feature: or the souvenir hunter who steals a fragment of an ancient building. It is the sense of glorious union which makes each part glorious: when a part is snatched the glory altogether departs. This may be compared to idolatry, in which some part is worshipped as the source of the splendour that belongs to the infinite whole. It is to infinitise the finite.

It was proposed in chapter three that in some mental illnesses sudden transitions take place from Scylla to Charybdis and back, from depression to mania, from a fixed obsessional paranoia to a chaotic psychotic state. These transitions were described as moving from one end to the other of a 'diabola', and are shown in the graph of Figure 3.1 (p. 39) as lines thrown across the Orthobola, the line of correlation.

We have again come upon Scylla and Charybdis as threats, not to mental health, but to the mystical journey. The first is to infinitise the finite, the second to finitise the infinite. In religious terms both are idolatrous. In the first, there is one fixed idol which is believed to be God. In the second, anything is regarded as God. Is there perhaps a mystical diabola from one to the other, from infinitising the finite to finitising the infinite, from idolatrous worship of a particular, to holding all particulars as divine?

There are dangers in exploring the Unconscious without a wise and experienced guide, and there are dangers in trying to draw near to God. The religious fundamentalist may cling to fixed thoughts of God, by which the infinite is reduced to the finite measure of conscious thinking. On the other hand there are emotional and ecstatic forms of religion in which emotional feelings are stirred up and indulged. These two dangers correspond again to Scylla and Charybdis respectively. The author of *The Cloud* warns that both thought and feeling must be laid aside together. Possibly the Orthobola may indicate a path that avoids both dangers, symmetric logic and unconscious depth are to be kept in proportion to one another. Symmetry without depth is chaos: depth without symmetry is idolatry.

6   The God of the Philosophers

In this chapter I shall argue that religious philosophies, and in particular the Scholastics, do not give information about a divine being who might be said to be 'conscious'. The 'God of the philosophers' is very similar to the mystics' God. They modify the concept of 'The Unconscious of God' only very little. The Consciousness of God remains elusive.

We now begin the search for the Consciousness of God. The search will be conducted within the language of faith. What more does this language require to be said of God than the paradoxical expressions of the mystical tradition? What does Christian faith require to be positively affirmed of God, which is not at once negatively contradicted?

Among those who have made positive affirmations about God are many who, in a narrow sense, are not Christian nor adherents of any traditional faith. The nature of ultimate reality has been debated by a great philosophical tradition, in the Western world as elsewhere. Faith, and theology, has often appropriated such philosophies to expound the roots of its own notion of God.

The theologian Paul Tillich refers at the beginning of his *Systematic Theology* to a number of philosophers of religion, as follows:

> In both the empirical and the metaphysical approaches ... it can be observed that the a priori which directs the induction and the deduction is a type of mystical experience. Whether it is 'being-itself, (Scholastics) or the 'universal substance' (Spinoza), whether it is 'beyond subjectivity and objectivity' (James) or the 'identity of spirit and nature' (Schelling) whether it is 'universe' (Schleiermacher) or 'cosmic whole' (Hocking), whether it is 'value-creating process' (Whitehead) or 'progressive integration' (Wieman), whether it is 'absolute spirit' (Hegel) or 'cosmic person' (Brightman) – each of these concepts is based on an immediate experience of something ultimate in value and being of which one can become intuitively aware ... The theological concerns of both idealists and naturalists are rooted in a 'mystical

a priori', an awareness of something that transcends the cleavage between subject and object.[1]

Tillich's own fundamental concept was 'Ultimate Concern for our being or non-being' and upon it he based his *Systematic Theology*. I have proposed that metapsychology might be used as the 'philosophical' basis for theology and in this the Unconscious will have a central role. It fits very well among the other '*a prioris*' in Tillich's list and fulfils the criteria he suggested: I have argued already that it is the ground or abyss in which is found mystical experience, the mystical *a priori*. The Unconscious, furthermore, is the source of human subjectivity, since from it comes all feeling. Yet since it is unknown and alien to our Consciousness, it appears to us as 'object', for in general our subjectivity is our Consciousness. The Unconscious therefore transcends 'the cleavage between subject and object' and the mystical path is an attempt to reach an awareness of this transcendence. Value and meaning are evidently determined by our emotions and feelings, not superficially, but in our most profound depths. Since it is the source of these, the Unconscious is clearly 'ultimate in value and meaning'.

Each of the philosophies mentioned by Tillich found some specific and thus asymmetric determination of the sheer emptiness of the ultimately symmetric. Having noted Tillich's belief that each is, at depth, standing on common ground, we may examine one of them at greater length. Within the Christian church by far the most influential of these philosophies is that of the Scholastics. Pride of place among the Scholastics belongs to Thomas Aquinas, whose philosophy since the papal encyclical of 1879, has been adopted as virtually normative for Roman Catholics. While few other Christians would regard his work so highly, his proofs of God's existence and his description of the 'attributes' of God have had a pervasive influence in Western Christianity.

Thomas Aquinas' God is certainly not 'beyond being and not-being'. On the contrary it is 'Being-itself'[2]. Therefore immediately there is an asymmetry, something asserted and not at once denied, and this is a first hint of something more than the Unconscious of God: it is a first hint of what 'the Consciousness of God' might mean.

Aquinas argued that God's existence is self-evident to natural reason, even unaided by supernatural revelation. He propounds five proofs of God's existence.[3] Each of these takes up a feature of created existence and argues that this feature must depend upon an ultimate something that is its source. These features are: motion, causality, possibility, gradation of properties, and purpose. The arguments are similar in each case and, particularly since it concerns

existence, the third will serves as an example. It runs as follows: since
any created thing comes into being and finally passes away, it has the
possibility of either being or not being. Its existence must therefore
depend upon something that was there before it. If this too was
created then the same applies to that; and so on back. Either, therefore, there is an infinite regress (which Aquinas says is impossible),
or there is something whose existence is a necessary fact, something
which does not come into being or pass away. This, Aquinas
concludes 'all men speak of as God'.

To modern ears the argument is not convincing, since there seems
no reason why things should not go back in an infinite regress –
unless it be a purely scientific reason such as scientific cosmology
now suggests in the theory of the 'Big Bang'. A reason of this kind
would be valueless to Aquinas, since it would rest on just another
empirical fact, a fact which further research might conceivably
disprove. It does not lead to something that could in principle not be
otherwise, something necessarily true.

This argument and the other four are collectively referred to as
cosmological arguments, since they proceed from the nature of the
world or cosmos. In *The Principles of Christian Theology*,[4] John
Macquarrie argues that the cosmological arguments are not really
rational arguments at all. Rather, they are ways of articulating an
awareness of the mystery of existence: they are expressions of the
capacity for contemplative wondering.

Mother Julian of Norwich, another of the fourteenth-century
English mystics, provides an excellent instance of such contemplative
wondering:

> God showed me a little thing the size of a hazel nut lying in the
> palm of my hand, and it seemed to me to be as round as a ball. I
> looked at it and thought, 'What can this be?', and I was answered
> thus, 'It is all that is made.' I marvelled how it could last because
> it seemed to me that it might fall suddenly to pieces because of its
> littleness. And I was answered in my understanding, 'it lasts and
> always will because God loves it'. And in the same way, everything
> has its being through the love of God.[5]

Mother Julian is presumably gazing at a real hazel nut. Its little-
ness and fragility as it rests in the palm of her hand suggests the
fragile nature of the things of time, upheld only by the love of God.
It would be a great misunderstanding to see the love of God
sustaining creation as a quasi-scientific energy: her vision is not of
such things, but of the contrast between what passes away and what
is eternal. Her perception is similar to that of Traherne, that 'som

thing infinite Behind evry thing appeared'.[6] A similar perception was
expressed by William Blake:

> To see a World in a Grain of Sand,
> And a Heaven in a Wild Flower,
> Hold Infinity in the palm of your hand,
> And Eternity in an hour.[7]

These perceptions do not provide argument for a particular being
behind the universe, whose action is required to explain its existence.
Contemplation of a grain of sand, a wild flower or a hazel nut can
induce a mystical experience of the infinite and the eternal, by
opening the door to the Unconscious. This may be called a perception of the mystery of existence, but that mystery is more a quality of
being, than an account of the origin of existence. Such perceptions
do not disclose the Consciousness of God – we are still in the eternal
territory of the Unconscious.

We may take, as a summary of what the cosmological arguments
provide, the famous assertion of Aquinas, that 'the being of creatures
is the doing of God'.[8] The means by which this doing takes place is
not, however, some scientific cosmological action that might put it in
rivalry with the 'Big Bang'. It is rather a perception of the infinite and
eternal which may be induced by contemplating any particular
creature. This contemplation induces an awareness, in scholastic
language, of a being's participation in Being-itself. Such perceptions
belong among those earlier described as 'transcendental experiences': in this case the perception of some particular thing as illuminated or endowed with the presence of the ultimate. Being-itself is
experienced in a being: the whole in a tiny part of it, which therefore
in bi-logical terms is symbolising the whole, through the modality of
symbolism. Cosmological arguments point primarily, therefore, to
the Unconscious of God, not to a divine actor setting off the 'Big
Bang' at the beginning of the universe.

The arguments of Aquinas have added to the mystics' God,
however, a distinctive characteristic, a touch of asymmetry. God is
not beyond being and non-being, but very definitely *is*, and all that is
has its being from it, though not in the way that a plain reading might
suggest.

If we follow Aquinas further in his account of that for which his
arguments provide evidence, we find ourselves in a discussion of the
'Attributes' of God. These are as near as most theologians will
advance towards a description of God, the indescribable, and are by
no means the property of Aquinas alone. They are variously listed by
different writers and are of the greatest interest for the argument of

this book: it was the strange coincidence that eternity is both an attribute of God and a characteristic of the Unconscious that set off our discussion in Chapter 1, and we shall now discuss the other attributes in the same spirit.

To recapitulate, the Unconscious of Freud is timeless and so, also, is God in his eternity. I borrowed Aquinas' quotation from Boethius who defined eternity as 'the instantaneously whole and complete possession of endless life'.[9] This ultimate form of eternity may be manifested in time in various penultimate forms, particularly the everlasting and the instantaneous. The Unconscious of God is purely eternal, the penultimate forms are the first hint of God's Consciousness.

Matte Blanco's theory allowed us to introduce alongside Freud's characteristics, a new one: placelessness or infinity. Likewise, God, according to the attribute of infinity, is to be neither placed nor bounded. He is beyond space, it is said: but not, of course, in a spatial sense of beyond – a paradox that renders the assertion all but meaningless! If we speak of him in relation to space, it would be necessary to say that space is in God, rather than God is in space. There is an exact parallel between the categories of eternity and infinity, time and space.

The penultimate forms are parallel also. For just as eternity gives birth in time to everlastingness, so infinity gives birth in space to ubiquity. God is everywhere in space or nowhere: in the penultimate form of the modality he cannot be in one place and not in another.

Freud's characteristics of displacement and condensation we amalgamated, with Matte Blanco's help, into the 'partlessness' of the Unconscious: the equivalence of part and whole, or of member and set. This too is an attribute of God, who has according to the Athanasian Creed,[10] no parts. Aquinas used the word 'simple' for this purpose. 'God then is altogether simple: there is in him no distinction of spatial parts, of form and matter, of nature and individuality etc.'. [11] In penultimate form, in relation to time and space, this means that if God is somewhere then God is wholly somewhere. As Aquinas wrote in his hymn about the presence of Christ in the Sacrament:

> Doubt not in each severed token,
> Hallowed by the word once spoken,
> Resteth all the true content.[12]

The whole Christ is present in the tiniest fragment of the consecrated bread – or he is not present at all. Likewise, since the logic is the same, if God is anywhere he is wholly there. If he is ubiquitous –

present everywhere – then he is wholly present everywhere, wholly present in every infinitesimal point of space.

The simplicity of God is apparently contradicted by the language of Scripture and by the imagery of the church. Such contradictions are evidently based upon images of God, generally images of God in human form. Where Christ speaks of the 'finger of God', or piety of 'the eye of God', it is his presence and his knowledge respectively that is implied. The anthropomorphisms are mere vehicles, not to be taken in any way literally.

The attribute of simplicity at first sight seems nonsensical. Yet there are certain parallels even with human consciousness. For example, though one part of me rather than another may be damaged, only I am in pain. We do not conceive normally of a part of me being in pain and another part not.[13] Pain – and other feelings – have a certain simplicity.

The simplicity of God is still better parallelled by the Unconscious, in which ultimately there can be no parts, for part and whole are totally identified (the modality of course of partlessness). Penultimately this creates symbolism. In extreme form the part is the whole, and the whole the part; in lesser degrees the part stands for the whole and is treated as it, and in weaker forms there is merely awareness of a likeness. This has already been discussed in its linguistic form in Chapter 4. The simplicity of God echoes the partlessness of the Unconscious, much as his eternity echoes its timelessness.

Another attribute of God is his ineffability. Strictly speaking, he cannot be spoken of. In ultimate form this silences the theologian utterly. This attribute may be compared with the modality of noncontradiction in the Unconscious. Speech that cancels out its assertions amounts to much the same as silence. Yet because God is not only his Unconscious, speech of a kind is allowed. There is first, and most symmetric, the koan of Zen Buddhism and the contradictions of all the mystics, wherein whatever is said must at once be unsaid. Penultimately, there is a strong paradox, whereby absolute contradiction appears to be expressed but ultimately avoided. Ante-penultimately, there are weaker paradoxes with only the appearance of contradiction. Alongside other penultimate forms Aquinas elaborated the principle of analogy. Scholastic debate had proposed the dilemma: were things said of God in the same sense as of created things or in a different sense? The latter possibility did justice to ineffability, but at the expense of comprehensibility: for if words used of God had a quite different meaning then how could anyone know what that meaning was? Yet if they had the same meaning this seemed to deny God's utter difference from creation and violated the attribute of ineffability. Aquinas' answer was the principle of analogy: words such as 'wise', for example, may be applied to God, but their meaning is proportioned to the difference between God and humanity. Thus the ineffable God may be spoken of, but only under severely restricted conditions. This modification of pure ineffability belongs among the penultimate forms of non-contradiction and thus gives a hint of the Consciousness of God.

Not usually classed as an attribute, but it may be discussed in their company, is Aquinas' contention that God is Pure Actuality. The meaning of this is simply that there are no possibilities in God or for God. Whatever is in God, is actual, already real. There can thus be no change in God, and nothing can affect him. There is nothing that he might or might not do: all God's acts are already eternally done. Pure Actuality in penultimate form becomes the attribute of omnipotence. Whatever happens in time is already present in God and decided by his eternal thought of it. Hence he is also omniscient, all-knowing. The attribute of impassivity is another expression of Pure Actuality: he can never be the passive partner in any transaction, since whatever happens is already in accordance with his eternal will.

Parallel to Pure Actuality is the fifth of Freud's characteristics. Reality and fantasy are indistinguishable to the Unconscious – what might be, is as real as what is. Whatever might be, once it is thought of, is as real as if it had taken place. Thus again, an Attribute of God is echoed by a Characteristic of the Unconscious.

The attributes of God therefore correspond very closely to the Freudian characteristics as modified and generalised by bi-logic. In ultimate form they describe the Unconscious of God. As these are unfolded or translated into the first hints of consciousness they take the penultimate forms of everlastingness, omnipresence, etc. Those first hints are still dominated by symmetry and the expressions of them by the modalities of language in strong forms.

In penultimate form God has a relationship to time and space, but it is a universal relationship. No particular creature is more or less thus related than any other. No particular event is more closely related to God than another. Thus far the God of philosophy has but little asymmetry and thus far, therefore, we can say little of the Consciousness of God.

Table 6.1 may summarise the discussion thus far.

The attributes of God are evidently close cousins, at the very least, of the characteristics of the Unconscious. What the mystic leaves behind the cloud of unknowing, the philosopher attempts to deal with by reasoned argument. If the philosopher's God is the same as the God of the mystics, or in any way like him, then the philosopher will have to speak of his or her God in the modalities imposed on

Table 6.1 The Characteristics of the Unconscious compared with the Attributes of God

Timelessness	Placelessness	Partlessness	Non-Contradiction	Non-reality
Ultimate forms in the Unconscious:				
Eternity	Infinity	Total Identity of part and whole	Co-presence of opposites	No distinction between truth and fantasy
Ultimate forms in God:				
Eternity	Infinity	Without parts	Beyond being and non-being	Pure Actuality
Penultimate forms in the Unconscious:				
Everlasting Momentary	Infinite extension Infinitesimal	Part treated as whole Whole treated as part	Irreconcilable paradox	Fantasy treated as truth and truth treated as fantasy
Penultimate forms in God:				
Everlasting	Ubiquitous	Wholly present wherever present	Ineffable	Omnipotent Omniscient Impassive

language by the Unconscious. These modalities are found in strongest form in verbal expressions of mental states close to the Unconscious, in transitional space. If the concept of God becomes less like the Unconscious it will be discussed in a correspondingly more asymmetric logic. Ultimate forms of the modalities will be replaced by penultimate forms and these in turn by statements that become more and more like those of rational speech. The God of the mystics is almost wholly symmetric. The God who acts in specific ways within time and space is clearly not. The Christian who thinks of God as personal, needs a God who analogically is both unconscious and conscious. He or she thinks of a God who is both the God of the mystics and also the God of revelation. In terms of the modalities, such a God is both eternal and temporal, infinite and finite, paradoxical and subject to common-sense logic. He will be spoken of symbolically, but the symbols may also be taken more literally. He will be spoken of in story. At times the story will be of the kind where reality cannot be distinguished from fantasy; and at times the story may be believed to be factually true – or false. To summarise these dichotomies, talk of God will sometimes be symmetric and some-times asymmetric and as a shorthand for this I have referred to a symmetric aspect of God and an asymmetric aspect, to the Unconscious of God and to his Consciousness.

The description of the Unconscious of God so far provided will be pursued here no further. It relies heavily upon the experience of the mystics amplified by the insight of the philosophers, particularly the Scholastics. The former modify the emptiness of the totally symmetric by the discovery of cosmic unity and love. The latter add to this an emphasis upon being and existence, to which we turn in the next chapter. After that will be discussed the yet more asym-metric aspect of God implicit in the notion of revelation.

7   Existence and Creation

The language of faith describes God as 'the creator'. This appears to point to an idea of God as a distinct being, who has 'done' something specific. Further examination suggests this is not the case: we find that the stories of creation are not about cosmology. Instead they affirm a certain vision of the relationship between the Unconscious and conscious thinking. If the Consciousness of God is to be found in them, it is not in what they describe, but in the stories themselves.

In the previous chapter we noted first the intimate parallels between the God of the mystics and the unrepressed Unconscious. The congruence between these seemed justified from both the religious and psychoanalytic perspectives. We moved on to the God of philosophical theism. The cosmological proofs of God's existence and the description of God in terms of his attributes appeared to point to the same congruence. That strand of the mystical tradition which experiences a sense of cosmic unity and love may be seen as fitting better with the Christian God than such strands as do not. This is a most important insight that will be developed later. However, the question that first must be addressed is whether this equation of the mystical and philosophical God with the Unconscious is adequate for the language of faith.

There is a long-running theological debate about whether a 'natural theology' is possible. By this is meant an account of God given by natural reasoning without the aid of revelation. Proofs of God's existence and descriptions of his attributes would generally be regarded as part of natural theology.

Some theologians, most notably in the twentieth century, Karl Barth, have argued that mere reasoning can never lead to God. He must always take the initiative in encounter with humanity and any God discerned purely by unaided human reason can only be an idol.

On this account knowledge of God comes only from his revelation of himself in Jesus Christ, which is known through his revealed word in the Bible. The great difficulty of this is that there seems then to be no way in which the word 'God' is to be understood. Who is it that is revealing himself? If no knowledge or explanation of 'God' apart from Jesus Christ is admissible, then what meaning can be given to the assertion that 'God' reveals himself through Jesus Christ?

It would seem that there must be something to be said of God prior to the claim that he is revealed in Jesus Christ, or that claim itself has no significance. Natural theology has attempted to provide that something. Yet another difficulty at once arises, for natural theologies have generally been couched in metaphysical arguments. These metaphysical arguments depended upon the existence of some agreed, or widely accepted philosophy. Plato, Aristotle, process philosophy and even existentialism in a sense, once provided the basis for such. All threw light upon the nature of being.

Metaphysics today is in an unhappy state. The shadow of Wittgenstein lies heavily upon the whole enterprise. In his *Philosophical Investigations*[1] he offered a therapy to dissuade philosophers from attempting it. One might picture metaphysics as a kind of architectural account of the universe which rests all other concepts upon a conceptual foundation-stone – such as those listed by Tillich.[2] Wittgenstein's therapy suggests that this is impossible. The meaning of what we say does not derive its validity from some single ultimate concept. On the contrary, meaning is disclosed by the use of words, and philosophical ultimates that have no use, are beating the air. If language is compared to a purposeful machine, they are like cogs that turn but do not engage with anything else and do not further the purpose of the machine. Our 'ordinary' language is essentially all right as it is; our thinking does not spring from some single ultimate concept; and so far from accounting for the true meaning of our words, it is those ultimate concepts themselves whose meaningfulness is questionable.

I propose then that the area of life in which the Unconscious of God is grounded is the mystical enterprise. Very many, who make no pretence to mysticism, yet have a sense of the eternal mediated through transcendental experiences. This is an area of life, therefore, of which such may have some understanding. In the present age no natural theology can do what might be required of it, but its place may be taken by the direct experience of 'the eternal'. It is this that 'locates' the word 'God' conceptually in human speech.

We might, nevertheless, by-pass Wittgenstein's therapy, if there was a generally agreed metaphysic to which natural theology could turn. In Chapter 2 I argued that in point of fact very many people use psychological concepts in place of those derived from metaphysicians or philosophers. Psychology, however, offers no account of being itself, of what it is for a thing to exist. In traditional metaphysical terms that is the department of ontology whereas psychology deals in phenomenology: how things appear, and more particularly how we appear to ourselves.

In traditional metaphysics, ontology is generally regarded as the prior question, and it is itself the crown of the whole enterprise. In a world without a metaphysic the question of being is unanswered. In the popular Western mind the physical sciences seem to have taken its place: if you ask what something *really* is, the answer is likely to involve atomic particles. God sits uneasily in their company.

To ask if God exists may seem a perfectly simple question, and one which many ordinary people debate. Conservative Christians are apt to demand of liberal Bishops a clear answer to the question. In the Sea of Faith movement there are those who, while claiming to be Christian, will affirm cheerfully that God does not exist. Neither side seems wholly aware of the problematic nature of the question itself, which lies in the word 'exist'. Lacking a generally agreed ontology, we have to resort to etymology to further the argument.

The *Shorter Oxford English Dictionary* holds that the word 'exist' is probably a 'back-formation' from the noun 'existence', a word derived from the Latin verb *existere*, the meaning of which is 'to emerge, be visible or manifest'. The root meaning of *existere* seems to be 'to stand out from'.

It is easy to see how a word with this derivation is applicable to physical objects – chairs, books and people – which if they do exist 'stand out' against their surroundings, or, if they do not exist, do not. We may, for example, reasonably ask whether the sun has a tenth planet beyond Pluto and so long as our definition of planet is sufficiently clear, the answer in principle is unambiguous. There will either be a tenth planet shining out of the night sky in the view of a suitable telescope, or there will not.

There are other kinds of thing for which the word 'existence' is applicable. For example, it makes sense to ask if unselfishness still exists in a materialist world. But if we ask if time exists, or if space exists, the question becomes more questionable. It is not in the least clear what either affirmation or denial would mean. There is nothing, except perhaps eternity and infinity, against which time and space can be said to 'stand out'.

In a similar way 'existence' is an unsuitable word etymologically to describe whatever reality the Unconscious has, since by definition the Unconscious is not visible or manifest and does not stand out from anything else. Likewise if we follow St Thomas Aquinas and the Scholastic tradition in describing God, not as a being, but as Being-itself, then again this seems unsuitable, for beings may emerge, or stand out of Being, but Being-itself does not stand out from anything, unless it be non-Being, and what purpose such an assertion would have is hardly clear.

The concept of God, as we have thus far discussed it, therefore seems to resist being coupled to the notion of existence at all. If God is no more than what I have called 'the Unconscious of God' then the logic appropriate to assertions about him is symmetric logic. In symmetric logic the proposition that he exists needs at once to be coupled with the assertion that he does not exist. One might want to say, 'No, the Eternal does not stand out from anything, it is that from which everything else stands out.' In other words, God does not exist himself, but is the giver of existence.

In so far as I have argued from etymology one might reasonably respond that etymology settles nothing – except purely etymological problems. Yet if that were so, one would expect to find another way of phrasing the question which did not suffer from the same objection. That is not as easy in this case as one might innocently expect.

The conservative, deprived of 'existence', may try 'reality'. 'Is your God real?', may be asked. But real is derived from the Latin res, and res means primarily a thing, object or being.[3] Etymologically, therefore, to assert the reality of God is to assert that he is a thing, and that is hardly correct from any theological perspective.

Deprived of 'reality' the conservative is not yet cornered. 'We demand that the Bishops affirm belief in a metaphysically objective theism', shrilly declared a well-known Anglican conservative. But again, 'objective' derives from 'object', and God is in no normal sense an object. And if one searches for a definition of theism, one will be returned inevitably to 'existence' and 'reality'. The problematic nature of metaphysics has already been noted.

The conservative seems to be driven back to the bare statement 'God is', which in English is barely grammatical at all – it would be odd to state 'The tenth planet of the sun is', if one meant by that that it existed.

We may concede that an etymological discussion of this sort does not settle anything; yet it does indicate that language is problematic in this respect, and that in turn suggests that the concept may be confused. I shall not attempt a discussion of 'existence' in, for example, the languages of Indian religion, which have far more sophisticated ways of discussing the existence of the divine. This wealth of language echoes a concept of the divine that is far more weighted to the mystical than is the God of Western Christianity.

Something of the same kind of difficulty arises in a discussion of the Unconscious. On the one hand, it has obviously no bodily existence: on the other, visible events and processes are said to be caused by it. In itself it might be called the unknowable background to the contents of consciousness, something at or beyond the horizon of ordinary awareness. The question of its ontological status is not important to most psychoanalysts and some prefer to talk simply of unconscious process, rather than of *the* Unconscious, for fear that this gives too substantial a feel to something essentially elusive.

To sum up, reifying language is inappropriate to the concept of God in so far as that concept corresponds to what I have called the Unconscious of God. This makes assertions about existence and reality inappropriate also. If these are to have meaning we must think of a God engaged within time and within space, with a God who 'does something'. Assertions about such a God may be handled with asymmetric logic – 'he does this, and not that'. A God of this kind would be analogically conscious as well as unconscious.

The argument in the church between 'realists' and 'non-realists' is an argument about the existence of God. Our discussion so far suggests that this is a nonsensical debate if the God in question is the infinite and eternal goal of the mystical journey or even the 'Being-itself' of the Scholastic philosophers (though within terms of their philosophy this claim would be rejected). If, however, there is, implicit in the language of faith, a concept of the Consciousness of God, as well as of the Unconscious of God, then these questions of existence may be applicable.

If faith does harbour a concept of the Consciousness of God, it will be expressed in assertions that are not subject to symmetric logic. It will be expressed in language not dominated by the modalities of the Unconscious in ultimate form. We need to look, therefore, for assertions that are not wholly paradoxical and negated by the first law of symmetric logic; or for assertions which are not at once to be reversed by the second law, or rotated by the third.

'IN THE BEGINNING' – THE CREATION STORIES

We turn then to the language of faith and may as well begin at the beginning, with God the creator. The Jewish and Christian Bible opens with the words:

> In the beginning God created the heavens and the earth. The earth was a vast waste, darkness covered the deep, and the spirit of God hovered over the surface of the water. God said, 'Let there be light', and there was light; and God saw the light was good, and he separated light from darkness.[4]

We find ourselves at once in a world of language apparently very different from that of the mystic. Our attention is directed to distinc-

tions and divisions, not to unities. The heavens and the earth are separated from one another, and light from darkness. Next, the waters
below the earth are to be divided from those above, the dry land from
the sea, the different kinds of plant will appear, and the different
heavenly bodies. Birds and fish and animals in all their distinct vari-
eties will appear and, finally, humankind, both male and female.

Out of whatever primal being that the Eternal has, time and space
and matter have come into existence, and all the distinct kinds of
creature that inhabit these. We are not told whether they have come
out of God, or out of nothing, or perhaps out of a primal chaos in
which nothing could be distinguished from anything else and about
which therefore no asymmetric logic could be applied. Moreover this
Creator is not indifferent to what has transpired – he speaks of it, sees
it, and observes that it is good. Whatever unimaginable life God had
'before', it is now a conscious God that we are invited to conceive of.
Asymmetry – matters spoken of in definite assertions – has emerged
from virtually total symmetry. Something definite is here being stated
about the ineffable.

We may look at the creator God in the light of the divine attributes.
His ineffability has been, at least, modified. His eternity is the ground
of what has taken place, but God is now also aware of change and
implicated in the events of time. His infinity may remain but in that
there now is what is not God, his infinity is, in a certain respect,
bounded. If we think of an image of God as an infinite ocean, there are
now, surrounded by this ocean, finite islands and their shorelines
constitute a boundary between them and God. The unimaginable and
inconceivable God is now symbolised through the image of a cosmic
craftsman who speaks and thinks, observes and judges. In each case
the ultimate form of a modality has become at most penultimate.

Yet we are by no means in the realm of the wholly asymmetric.
The act of creation is not to be given a date. In 1654, Archbishop
Ussher famously computed it at 4004 BC but that year is of no more
theological significance than Professor Hawking's 15 billion BC,[5] for
if time and space were created together with the first creatures, the
act of creation took place at no specific time and at no specific place.
It seems abundantly clear that we cannot literally take the first
chapter of Genesis as the description of an event. Rather it is a
description of a relationship between creature and creator that is true
at any time or place. Furthermore, although distinctions are clear
between one creature and another, the relationship of each to the
creator is thus far the same as that of any other. Creatureliness is a
universal property. Therefore, symmetry is still dominant in this
story, for it is a timeless, placeless story of universal application. Even
though it might be called an account of the birth of asymmetry, it is

in strongly symmetric terms. Moreover, if we read on to Genesis 2 we find a second account of creation, which at many points is in contradiction to the first: God creates in one day, not in seven. He creates not out of a watery chaos, but a dusty desert; he creates not male and female humans together, but one male, etc. In this second account, God is more clearly endowed with human features. He not only speaks and observes, but forms man out of dust like a potter. He is altogether more anthropomorphic. The Eternal God is symbolised as a being in human form. The biblical account of creation is thus expressed through the modalities of timelessness, spacelessness, paradox and symbolism.

The fifth modality is the equivalence of fantasy and reality. Since in these two stories we are clearly dealing with something that no eye has seen, no ear has heard, nor any witness recorded, the usual tests of historical truth are inapplicable. These stories are the work of the human imagination. Only an extreme fundamentalist could take them for fact. Yet Christian theology does not therefore dismiss them as mere falsities. They convey something to which faith is committed which is not to be limited to the categories of historical truth or falsehood. They share many properties therefore with those stories which in an individual psychoanalysis would be called fantasy: a story powerfully at work, determining behaviour and vision of life, yet whose influence is not dependent upon factual truth. Such is the nature of myth, in the proper sense, not an untruth, but a story beyond the classification into false and true that is appropriate for determinable past history.

The creation story appears at first sight to be couched in assertions subject to asymmetric logic. Further examination, however, reveals the pervading presence of the modalities of speech which indicate the underlying influence of symmetric logic. Nevertheless, in the quest for an asymmetric aspect of God we have found something. For example, the assertion that 'God made man in his own image' is not to be subjected to symmetry – for that would deliver the assertion that 'man made God in his own image', an assertion made by Feuerbach, the nineteenth-century atheist, and rejected by theology in general as an assault upon its ultimate foundation. In short, in the terms introduced in Chapter 3 we may place the creation stories in the region of the Orthobola that I have called transitional space.

UNREPRESSED UNCONSCIOUS AND TRANSITIONAL SPACE – FIFTH MODALITY

Transitional space has been described in Chapter 3 as the zone of mental life, which, while to a degree conscious is yet strongly marked by unconscious characteristics. There are asymmetries, but symmetry is still very strong. The logic and language of this zone has been described with the help of the rhetorical figures of speech in Chapter 4. In this zone the Unconscious unfolds into Consciousness; Consciousness attempts, in Matte Blanco's term, to translate the contents of the Unconscious.

What are these 'contents'? Our attention so far has been primarily addressed to the ultimate depth of the Unconscious which has been identified with the goal of the mystic – and it would be stretching language to call this a 'content' at all. The Unconscious contains also elements of repressed consciousness, the main focus of Freud's work. These are the buried memories which resistance holds away from Consciousness, and which generally exercise a baleful influence upon it. Since they are both deeply unconscious but also to a degree asymmetric, they are a major constituent of the Scylla which lies 'above' the Orthobola. What then can we say of the unrepressed Unconscious that is more specific than its ultimate depth?

Since the Unconscious has been described as timeless, it might be objected that it can have no contents at all, which were not there 'from the beginning'. Yet repressed conscious contents have clearly arisen from experiences having a definite time and place. Therefore the whole Freudian tradition allows some modification of absolute timelessness, within the sphere of the Unconscious. Temporal events somehow *can* move into the zone of timelessness; once there, however, they are relatively unchanging and are marked by the characteristics and modalities that have been described.

The question that next arises is whether there are other contents besides those arising from repression. In other words, does the *unrepressed* Unconscious have content? And if so, what might be the nature of this content?

Matte Blanco devotes considerable space to discussing Freud's treatment of these questions and concludes that, while Freud clearly implies that there is an unrepressed Unconscious, he is less than clear about its nature and contents.[6] Certainly fantasies are present to the Unconscious, but are all fantasies based upon repressed material?

Carl Jung believed Freud had unduly limited psychology by making repressed material his main focus of attention. He distinguished two main levels in the Unconscious. The first, the personal Unconscious, mainly contained repressed material: but the second and deeper, the collective Unconscious, had inherited contents of the greatest significance:

> there exists a second psychic system of a collective, universal, and impersonal nature which is identical in all individuals. This collective unconscious does not develop individually but is inherited. It

consists of pre-existent forms, the archetypes, which can only become conscious secondarily and which give definite form to certain psychic contents.[7]

When the archetypes become conscious they take shape in images and symbols, the shadow, the *anima*, the wise old man or woman, the rock, and so forth, which while expressed differently in each individual or in each culture, yet arise from the same fundamental archetypal form. Jung regarded these as immensely important and the bulk of his writings are about them.

But Freudians too have written of the contents of the unrepressed Unconscious. Bruno Bettelheim, for example, was an orthodox Freudian who specialised in work with emotionally disturbed children. In his very well-known book, *The Uses of Enchantment*, he discussed the role of fairy stories in the emotional development of the young. He argued that fundamental fears and hopes natural to different stages of growing up are addressed unconsciously by fairy stories, providing reassurance and affirmation.

> For example, many fairy stories begin with the death of a father or mother; in these tales the death of the parent creates the most agonising problems, as it (or the fear of it) does in real life …
>
> It is characteristic of fairy stories to state an existential dilemma briefly and pointedly. This permits the child to come to grips with the problem in its most essential form.[8]

Repetition of the story gradually allows it to engage with the inner and unconscious life of the child, and it would seem an obvious conclusion that the story becomes a part of the child's Unconscious, linked, as Bettelheim made clear, both to repressed and *to other* unconscious contents.[9] The story is of course consciously entertaining, but it is also working beneath the surface, caught into the zone of the Unconscious.

The means by which such stories work illustrates some of the themes of Chapter 4. A typical opening is, 'long, long ago', hinting at eternity. Events take place 'in a faraway land', hinting at infinity. All characters, says Bettelheim, 'are typical, rather than unique':[10] which is to say that they readily permit a symbolic meaning – the third modality. Most importantly, they permit the hearer to identify him- or herself with the central character. It is above all this feature which allows them to work unconsciously. Paradox is expressed in the miraculous: eggs that are made of gold, wolves who turn out to be grandmothers, etc. Such features reinforce the sense of fantasy: but yet the story is absorbed in a very serious spirit. It is clearly real to the child on some level – the level of 'existential dilemma'. The distinction between fantasy and reality is thus evidently not to be drawn. The story has engaged with the Unconscious and become absorbed into its unrepressed contents.

Bettelheim raises the question of the kind of reality that belongs to a fairy story. His approach may be illustrated in this way:[11] if a frightened child asks, 'Are there really giants around?', which might be interpreted as 'Do giants exist?', the proper answer is not, 'No, they are just fictional', but rather, 'Yes, but not near here.' The former answer is improper because it does not address the real question: it merely deprives the child of a symbolic expression of his or her fears. It therefore baffles the child and possibly deepens the anxiety, because it is now rendered inaccessible to verbal reassurance. The proper answer accepts the child's symbolic framework and may bring relief; of course, sometimes the child will prefer his or her own opinion and remain frightened. The dialogue, however, thus conducted takes place on an appropriate playing field. The adult has not vandalised the child's symbols.

Bettelheim draws a sharp distinction between fairy story and myth. The former is essentially optimistic, the giants are defeated, the wicked stepmother disgraced, and the protagonists live happily ever after. In contrast, the tone of myths is pessimistic. The tragic hero, Oedipus or Orestes, is overcome by fate and ultimately destroyed. Yet even though the message is very different, the medium is strikingly similar. The stories are set long ago and often, though not necessarily, in another place. The hearer is again invited to identify with the protagonist, and deep existential dilemmas are addressed.

For an account of the beginnings of myth we may turn to the great anthropologist, Mircea Eliade. He discusses not the tragic heroes of the developed world of ancient Greece, but the stories of prehistorical, primordial humanity.

In Eliade's view[12] the myths of primordial peoples took place in a time before time, which he calls the 'Great Time'. They are set in an unidentified place, or one far away. They describe on this wider canvas those activities which were central to the life of primordial humanity. The great Hunter goes out to hunt and kills his prey. The Creator prepares the ground and plants the first seeds. Fire is tamed for human purposes. When people hunted, planted or made fires they were re-enacting the acts of the gods or heroes in the Great Time. They did not merely imitate them: they actually themselves became these archetypal figures. This identification characterises the third modality (symbolism), in what I have called its ultimate form.

Furthermore, Eliade argues that, to primordial humanity, life was only meaningful when it was a re-enactment of myth. Any part of life that was not such a re-enactment had no reality or existence. Participation in the Great Time alone gave life significance. Only by total identification with the mythical archetypes did people perform real actions.

If there was any way one could ask a primordial hunter whether the great Hunter had really slain his prey in the Great Time, one can only suppose that the question would be meaningless and inappropriate. The primordial hunter knew that the great Hunter killed again whenever he himself had a successful day. The past existence and reality of the great Hunter could not meaningfully be questioned, for it was he who gave existence and reality to the present time.

Bettelheim and Eliade both speak of stories in another time, whose reality is unquestionable, and with which the hearer identifies. The stories are told again and again and, while obviously received consciously, appear also to be speaking to the Unconscious, in which they become embedded. Questions of empirical reality are thus quite inappropriate: they function in the fifth modality, where story and reality are not to be distinguished.

There seems then a strong case for talking of the contents of the unrepressed Unconscious. Such contents partake to a degree of timelessness, though some movement is possible. Stories may enter these contents, or at least engage with them. Stories may cease to engage on this level, suggesting that the contents have changed, or other facets of the content have become dominant. Stories may lie dormant, and may reawaken in relation to the fears or drives or hopes of a later stage of growing up – in which they may have a quite different significance.

By recognising the presence of the fifth modality in the creation story we are bringing it into parallel with the fantasies which, lodged in the mind perhaps from early years, shape and influence the individual's life and disposition. Whether such stories are empirically true or false is less important than that they are thus lodged. Whether the events which the stories depict actually happened or not is unimportant in the therapy of the individual, if therapy is needed. The stories are there, and through the repetition of them something of the present state of the person is expressed and revealed. In a parallel way the empirical truth of the creation story cannot be ascertained and hardly matters. The story is lodged in the mind of faith as an expression of how creation is seen, valued and treated, an expression of a relationship between humankind and God.

In support of this view and at risk of flogging a dead horse, it is noteworthy that St Thomas Aquinas himself admitted the possibility that creation was everlasting, and that its created nature would in no way be changed by this. Only because he took the book of Genesis to supply empirical evidence did he believe creation had a definite beginning. Likewise the latest cosmology favours a 'Big Bang' theory of the beginning of the universe, but not long ago a theory of continuous expansion and contraction pointed to an everlasting universe: yet few if any Christians abandoned belief in creation upon that basis.

In defence of religion against the advance of science, conservative Christians have at times pointed to gaps in scientific theory and claimed these as spaces in which the action of God may be discerned. Such gaps have been the beginning of the universe, the coming about of life, the development of human consciousness and the relationship of mind and matter. Since science continually advances, such a 'god of the gaps' is a shrinking god. His relationship to creation becomes ever more tenuous and the links made between what science cannot yet explain and what the Bible appears to claim are ever more stretched. Scientific cosmology no longer needs such a god 'to start things off', and if it did, it would bear very little relationship to the god of the first chapter of Genesis. If the biblical God is to remain important, it will not be as a solution to a problem in cosmology.

The god of the gaps is a product of a reductionist way of thinking, in the terms described in the Introduction. Creation was not in seven days, but in 15 billion years. It was not the ordering of a watering chaos but the initiation of the 'Big Bang', and so forth. All the details slide away, while an attempt is made to rescue a single alleged fact – God created the world.

But what is the content of this alleged fact? What does it actually mean? The notion of 'creating' or 'making' the world is surely a metaphor derived from those activities in which objects of use or beauty are fashioned out of raw materials, the work of a potter or a carpenter. The difficulty is to say what event or process the metaphor exists to describe. If it is an event 'at the beginning' then we are involved in the territory of the scientific cosmologist – who might with another twist of the scientific argument return to an everlasting universe. On the other hand, to describe the universe as created might be a way of describing a quality of its actual present nature. But this produces further difficulties. That quality might be something within the range of science – but that returns us to a 'god of the gaps'. If it is not a scientific matter, it might be a philosophical necessity. That would be a return to a metaphysical ontology – a theory of being. However, I have already suggested that there is no commonly accepted ontology to which one might appeal, apart possibly from the implicit ontology of a scientific outlook. It could, of course, be the case that there is an ontology yet to be discovered by philosophy: but few philosophers offer much hope of that, at least in the tradition descending from Wittgenstein. That tradition offers powerful arguments for the view that all attempts to construct such an ontology are doomed.

What is it then that faith understands by describing the universe as created? I propose a double answer to this question. First, any object may be the focus of a transcendental experience, of the type Traherne, Mother Julian or Blake describe. Through any particular object a sense of the coherence and wonder of the whole universe may be bestowed. It is this sense which the cosmological argument for God's existence expresses, and indeed may evoke. In the Christian tradition such experiences are sometimes described as experiences of the created nature of the universe. This leads to the second part of the answer. To understand the universe as created is to testify to the power of the creation stories of Scripture. A story has power to the extent that it is engaging the Unconscious. When the creation stories do that, they are operating in transitional space beyond the divide between fantasy and reality. They cannot therefore be reduced to fact, and indeed resist the attempt to do so. Because the Christian has received these stories at this level, transcendental experiences of the type described are likely to be interpreted in terms suggested by these stories. Furthermore they will condition the feelings and values held towards 'the created universe'. When such a phrase as 'created universe' is used it is not the assertion of a fact, but a shorthand that points to the stories in all their mythic detail, and to the possibility of an insight into the cosmic unity sensed in certain transcendental experiences.

Our search for the Consciousness of God in stories of the beginning has not led us to identify some distinct act of God either at the beginning of time, nor in the sustaining of things in existence. It has led us to the creation stories themselves. If there is an act of God to be discovered it is in the forming of these stories over many centuries, in their transmission and in their telling today. Such a conclusion is entirely orthodox, for God is above all known, not as a god of the gaps, but through his revealed word. This revealed word is not to be reduced to fact, neither in the literal way of the fundamentalist, nor in the apparently more sophisticated manner of the reductionist. It should be allowed to be, and exert its influence in transitional space without any attempt to translate it into alleged fact.

I have already introduced the word 'myth' to describe stories operating in transitional space. The word is not to be understood in the journalistic sense of an 'untruth'. There are many more erudite definitions of it, but I will use it to refer to those stories involving God which are shaped by the fifth modality. Such stories should not be seen as empirically true *or* false, for they belong in transitional space where fantasy and reality are equated. The important question is not their relationship to the factual and empirical, but whether or not they are lodged in the mind at the level of transitional space. Then the one who hears the myth will be receiving it in the manner which its own construction demands: expressions of eternity and infinity, symbols, and paradoxes will be received as such. If a myth is not heard in this way, then the modalities – especially that of paradox – will deliver obstacles to the comprehension of the rational mind, instead of providing lures and stimulations to the depths of the imagination.

Over against the myths of Genesis as their appropriate rivals are not the scientific cosmologies, but perhaps the myth forming in Job's mind when he wonders if the world has not been made in utter malice to torment him and the other human victims of its creator. Or the Gnostic notion that the Eternal, the utterly symmetric, has no relationship to creation at all, which instead is the work of a funda- mentally evil 'Demiurge', a malevolent being intermediate between the Eternal God and creation. Or again the mythical vision prevalent in classical culture of a Fate which arbitrarily and meaninglessly predetermines the events of human life.

None of these competing stories is to be challenged on the basis of empirical evidence. Each of them communicates and expresses a world-vision which, if deeply lodged unconsciously, will determine one's experience in contrasting ways. To assess the biblical stories of the beginning as mythical is not to marginalise them, but to release them in their full power and glory.

Where the creeds speak of the Creator, or a theologian speaks of a created universe, they should not be understood as speaking of facts towards which the narratives crudely point. On the contrary, these terms are signposts to the narratives. Those which are picked out in this way by the creeds may be seen as having, within the whole text of Scripture, a specially important status.

We began this chapter in search of the Consciousness of God. We were looking for an activity of God about which faith makes asser- tions that are not subject primarily to symmetric logic. We have not found such activity in the creating of the world, but instead have found certain great stories which faith uses in a mythical, and thus mainly symmetric manner. If we have found anything of the Consciousness of God, it is not in some cosmic act, but in the stories which tell of such acts, stories formulated over centuries in the imag- ination of humankind. Thus far the stories themselves are all that we have found.

8 Justice and Choice

We continue the search for the Consciousness of God. The biblical history of Israel appears to be about the actions of a divine being who chose a particular people and demanded justice from them. In choice and justice we find the unfolding of the Unconscious. We find this unfolding to be the principal mode of divine action: what appear to be described as divine interventions in history are actually treated as myths to express this unfolding. Historically, if there is a 'work of God' here, it is the making of the myth.

The Jewish and Christian Scriptures begin with the account of creation. In the previous chapter we have interpreted this story as myth expressing the emergence of the many from the One, of asymmetry coming out of symmetry. It is an account in mythic form of the Unconscious unfolding into Consciousness We noted, too, that the mystics have spoken of a sense of cosmic unity in their experience of the One. Scripture speaks of a God who controls history; if he does so, perhaps it is through this sense of cosmic unity, and, therefore, I shall now attempt to trace the impulsion towards cosmic unity in the biblical history. In particular two themes emerge, choice and justice. Choice, because an awareness of God brings a sense of a special relationship with God, of the unity between a particular one and the One; justice, because the justice of God demands right relationship between his creatures – the symmetry of the One may be expressed in a harmony between the many. Choice is important because, ideally, the desire for unity with the One imparts a desire to express the symmetry of the One in justice between the many. Yet it is often distorted into a desire for a special closeness to the One, regardless of others, and thereby leads to injustice and fratricide.

The first creation story describes the making of humankind on the sixth day, along with other inhabitants of the dry land:

Then God said, 'Let us make human beings in our image, after our likeness ...' (Genesis 1:26)

God created human beings in his own image;
in the image of God he created them;
male and female he created them. (Genesis 1:27)

In the second creation story, we read:

The Lord God formed a human being from the dust of the ground
and breathed into his nostrils the breath of life so that he became
a living creature. (Genesis 2:7)

This living creature is thereafter named Adam, and may be translated
as simply 'the man'. He – for he is a male – is put in the Garden of Eden
at the centre of which there is a tree, the tree of life. The story is
confusing at this point for it is not clear whether there are two trees,
the tree of life, and the tree of the knowledge of good and evil, or not.
Scholarly debate gives us no certain conclusion, as to whether the two
trees arise from the conflation of two different stories, or not. The
theme of a single central tree is one of great antiquity and found in the
myths of many nations. It stands at the centre of the universe, the place
at which the events of the Great Time take place.[1] It is one of many
signs that the story which unfolds is taking place in transitional space.

God observes that the man is alone: this is not good and so the
animals and birds are made to keep him company. The man gives
them names as each is brought before him and we may see in this a
parallel account to the creation of animals in the first chapter.
However, here it is not God who is becoming aware of the distinc-
tiveness of the many, but the man. Here is a story of the beginning
of asymmetry in the human mind. Yet the intention is to find one in
whom man may find a unity, a return to symmetry. The animals do
not fulfil this aim and so in the total symmetry of a deep sleep, God
takes from Adam a rib, and fashions it to be the first woman, flesh
from his flesh, bone from his bone – in order that the two might
become one. The longing of Adam for one with whom he may be one
is the longing of the particular for a return to the unity of the One.
This return is not a direct return to the One, but a return to the One
through another – for their mutual harmony will be expressive of the
symmetry of the One, while at the same time their particularity will
not be done away.

The man and woman live together apparently in a perfect
harmony with the ideal world in which they are set, with one another
and with God. This unimaginable perfection has to us a dream-like
quality. We are still in a world dominated by symmetry. There is one
discordant note, however: God has issued a very clear and asymmetrical command, one which in no way incorporates its opposite, that
the couple may not eat from the fruit of the tree. Tempted by a

snake, they disobey, and the dream breaks up. The decline began with the eating of the forbidden fruit. Its effect upon Adam and Eve was that 'the eyes of both were opened, and they knew that they were naked':[2] they became, as God said, 'like one of us, knowing good and evil'.[3] The opening of eyes suggests a movement towards consciousness and it issued in the ability to make distinctions. This ability implies an exercise of asymmetry – such and such is good, not evil: such and such else is evil; not good. However, in becoming like God, they also gained the potential to be infinite and eternal. God perceived this threat and ejected them from the Garden of Eden to circumvent it. Verse 22 continues:

> and now, lest he put forth his hand and take also of the tree of life, and eat, and live for ever.

The aposiopesis expresses God's infinite dismay – or anger? – at the possibility of humankind sharing his infinity. Such a reversal at this stage would amount to the One reabsorbing the many: time and history would never come to be. There is a psychological parallel in the individual life with the infantile temptation to refuse to grow up, to be eternally fused with the mother.

Adam and Eve at once experience an awakening to sexual desire and after their act of intimacy become aware of their nakedness and of shame. Their sexual difference and separateness is thrust upon their attention. Asymmetry has obtruded in a new and more forceful way. God descends to punish their presumption and they are driven out of the garden of innocence into a hostile world of real things. From this point on, the conflicts between the dream of harmonious symmetry and the reality of struggle between the particulars of creation will haunt humankind.

The many have come from the One, but they come with a longing for the One, a longing which can be distorted into a longing to be the One. God permits Adam to have a partner and wills that with her he will live in harmony, since she is 'bone of his bone' and 'flesh of his flesh'. Such harmony might have been an image of the eternal symmetry of the One: 'in his image and likeness created he them'. However, when Adam tries to become the One through eating the fruit, he is rejected, for this is a forbidden return to the One, a return in which the individual one seeks to become the One. It is forbidden because it is a retreat from the multiplicity of creation: the one who becomes the One has no need of any other, and, for that one, creation might as well not be.

There is a fundamental conflict between the dream of being the One and the true path to unity with the One. It takes a very clear form in the rivalry of the first couple's sons, Cain and Abel. The rivalry arises from an apparently arbitrary act of God who accepts Abel's offering while rejecting Cain's. The Bible offers no explanation of this arbitrariness. Both appear to be worthily returning thanks to the creator. We may speculate that if every sacrifice is acceptable, then no notion of acceptability arises. In a world of asymmetric distinction acceptance, even love, can only be perceived by an awareness of their opposites. Thus a choice has to be made: one has to be loved, another rejected. Perhaps on another day Cain would have been the favoured one: he did not wait for another day and murdered his brother instead. The constraint of time in which one person can do only one thing at a time (even if he is God!), causes apparent injustice and thus seems to deny the eternal embrace of love.

This story is the archetypal struggle between siblings for parental love, foreshadowing what was to come in Genesis between Isaac and Ishmael, Jacob and Esau, Joseph and his brothers. The sacrificial offering is a communion sacrifice, a means of identification with God, of claiming sonship, of being holy. The danger that lies in any communication with God is of seeking to be God. Cain finds himself first rejected, then driven by this rejection to murder: consequently cursed and sentenced to a life of wandering, alienated from 'the centre'. By trying to become the sole heir, Cain has repeated the attempt of Adam and Eve to become one with God. By killing he has removed the threat to being One implicit in the existence of another. God again rejects the one who tries to be the One and thus God protects the coming to be of the many: for all at once we find Seth appearing, another, thus far unheard of, brother. Yet though Cain is rejected, he is not destroyed. Instead God threatens seven-fold revenge against anyone who slays him and a mark of protection is put on his head. Is this to prevent Seth, as sole remaining heir, becoming identified with the One? Or is it because God recognises his own guilt in driving Cain to murder through that first arbitrary choice?

For whatever reason, the danger of the one particular becoming the One is warded off and Cain and his new brother Seth have children and the human race multiplies. However, the same conflict remains. This is next exemplified in Lamech, a descendent of Cain. He boasts:

I have slain a man for wounding me, a young man for striking me.
If Cain is avenged sevenfold, truly Lamech seventy-sevenfold.[4]

This is a boast of psychopathic arrogance. Lamech construes any attack on himself as justifying killing in return. Any attack on himself, one may suppose, is equated by him symmetrically with a murderous

attack and therefore justifies murderous response: symmetry is operating malignly. The reason for this follows. Where God was content
with seven-fold revenge for Cain, with whom he had identified
himself by putting his mark on him, Lamech demands seventy-seven
fold. The hyperbole suggests infinity, and the effect of the boast is of
Lamech identifying himself with God – and more than God: the individual, Lamech, is identifying himself with the One.

Lamech's son was Noah and in his days God seems to have been
tempted to imitate Lamech. God saw that 'the wickedness of man
was great in the earth and that every imagination of the thoughts of
his heart was only evil continually'[5] and he resolved to destroy everything without distinction. Yet in the end a saving asymmetry inter-
vened, since God made a distinction between Noah and the rest of
humankind, choosing to discriminate between the righteous and the
unrighteous.

Noah, warned by God, builds an ark and gathers into it his own
family and representatives of every species upon earth. Then the
flood begins. It is much more than a flood, however: it is a mingling
of the waters above with the waters below, an undoing of God's work
on the second day of creation. Once more the earth becomes a vast
waste. There are no particulars left and there is a return to total
symmetry, except within the Ark. Had God not saved the Ark, the
many would have passed away and only the One remained.

When all is destroyed, the waters gradually subside and the Ark
comes to rest on a mountain top. Mountains, like trees, are symbols
of 'the centre'. Noah, his family and the animals with him leave the
Ark, spread out from this new centre, and multiply in what is effectively a new creation. God then promises never again to destroy the
earth in such a way and gives the rainbow as a sign of this new
covenant. The One commits itself to the existence of the many, even
though they may be 'wicked'.

A second decline set in. It began once more with a distinction
between brothers. Noah became drunk and fell asleep naked. Ham
went in and saw his father's nakedness. Graced with more respect, his
two brothers went in backwards, so as not to see their father's shame,
and covered him with a garment.[6] Ham was then cursed by Noah,
Shem and Japheth were blessed. Ham was to be their slave and, therefore, outside the covenant community that later was to be established.
The decline continued and in the story of the Tower of Babel we are
told that God again felt threatened by the infinite possibilities of
human achievement, as he had been when Adam and Eve had access
to the fruit of the forbidden tree. God came down and scattered the
nations, confusing their language, so that they could not succeed in
building a tower to reach into the heavens and thereby take his place.

Having thus broken the unity of humankind by asymmetric division into separate peoples and languages, God adopted a new strategy to combat human inclination to claim divinity. He chose Abraham and his descendants to be his own people. Like Abel asymmetrically chosen from the rest, he chose them to be the object of a symmetric identification of himself with them, expressed in the chiasmus:

I will bless those who bless you
and him who curses you, I will curse.[7]

Or as tradition later expressed it:

I will be your God
and you will be my people.[8]

In our search for the consciousness of God this is a defining moment. The act of choosing one from the many, as we have already seen in the story of Cain and Abel, is an asymmetric assertion: this one is chosen, those – or that one – are not. These acts of choice by God are central to the thought of the Scriptures and dominate the unfolding of God's will in history as they record it.

We find then a *prima facie* conflict between the notion of asymmetric choice by God, and the notion of a universal justice willed by God, springing from the symmetry of the Unconscious of God. The Scriptures are very largely an account of how the descendants of Abraham wrestled with this conflict. On the one hand lay the Scylla of seeing this choice as for their benefit alone: of identifying the will of God with the success of his people. This is to see God, the universal One, as 'our God' and not 'their God as well'. It is to see the One as a particular one. It limits the One by an asymmetric assertion ('the One is *our* God'), thus treating the ultimate Unconscious as less than wholly symmetric – which is the rock of Scylla in the graph of Figure 3.1 (p. 39) – finitising the infinite. On the other hand lay the Charybdis of forgetting the choice altogether, of merging with the surrounding peoples and adopting their multiplicity of gods. Since each such god is finite, limited by its peers, this is to infinitise the finite, to treat many particular gods with the symmetry that belongs to the One. This falls in the area of the graph described as the whirlpool of Charybdis.

Between these errors – which amount to claiming to know either too much about God or too little – and transcending both, lay the true insight. Choice is not for the good of the chosen alone, but is God's strategy for bringing about universal blessing: if God reveals himself as 'our God', he is also in the end equally 'their God' as well.

At the beginning Abraham is told that 'through him will every family on earth be blessed'. Nevertheless, again a choice is made by God between the first son, Ishmael, the son of the slave-girl Hagar, and Isaac, the son of Abraham's wife, Sarai. Ishmael and Hagar are cast out into the desert to die of hunger and thirst: it is hard to see at first how they are to share in universal blessing. Yet the divine love is shown to them and they are rescued by an angel, and Ishmael fulfils his destiny to become the father of another nation.

Again, in the next generation, Jacob, the younger and weaker son, by trickery obtains his brother Esau's birthright and deprives him of the unique paternal blessing. Jacob, known also as Israel, becomes the channel of election, while Esau is displaced. Yet he, too, becomes the father of another nation.

These choices between brothers are used by the Israelite tellers of these stories to define, not only God's choice, but national relationships with neighbouring peoples, Ishmaelites, Edomites and the rest. With these Israel was often in conflict and the stories may have served a purpose in justifying this: yet they were also reminders that the enemy was originally a brother. The identification of oneself with the other, essential for mutual justice, was still enjoined.

Jacob, or Israel, became the father of twelve sons, the eponymous ancestors of the twelve tribes. Again there is strife between them and Joseph, apparently his father's favourite, is sold into slavery in Egypt by his older brothers. After various vicissitudes he emerges as next only to Pharaoh himself and when Palestine is afflicted by famine, the saviour of his brothers and his father. All this is within the scope of God's elected people, yet it foreshadows another important theme: the chosen one is rejected, suffers, and through this becomes the saviour of his persecutors.

The whole clan settle in a part of Egypt and multiply until they are a nation, whereupon their hosts become threatened by them and they are enslaved. It appears God's choice is forgotten, but Moses, whose life is providentially preserved in infancy, is raised up to revive their fortunes. His first efforts to secure justice are unsuccessful and he flees from Pharaoh to the wilderness. There, in a mystical and transcendent experience, God discloses himself to Moses. He is the God of Abraham, the God of Isaac and the God of Jacob. Scholarly speculation has wondered whether these were originally three separate gods. Whether he is one or three, the God who speaks to Moses offers a new answer. He is not to be identified merely through the choice of an ancestor, for that lends itself too easily to an identifying of a particular one with the One: it is too particular and potentially exclusive. Instead of giving a specific name at all, he proclaims 'I am who I am', or possibly 'I will be what I will be'; either translation is possible.

Moses returns and finally leads his people out of Egypt into the desert to become, at last, God's chosen people. In the desert Moses ascends a mountain and receives the law under which the people are to live. This is another moment of the greatest importance in the biblical story. By living in accordance with the law, the people will be responding to God's choice of them as the channel of blessing for all humankind. In the law, therefore, it is revealed how the many are to live in accordance with the will of the One. We must therefore now note certain crucial features of the law.

First of all it is in the form of a covenant, a treaty, between God and his people. They are offered a choice as to whether they will accept God's choice of them in this form. The purpose of the covenant is to bind the many to the One. There are provisions for the worship which will express this. The Israelites are not to confuse the One with any created particular, for that would lead them to Scylla. Nor are they to worship other gods as well, for then they would be in Charybdis. They are to worship only the One, with whom they identify themselves especially through sharing the sabbath rest at the end of the first week of creation. They are to make no image of the One – for that risks confusing some one thing with the One. They are to treat the revealed name of the One with awe in case it is trivialised. Such laws – and many others – define how the many relate to the One. These laws express the theme of 'choice'.

The law contains far more than this, however. It defines also how the many are to relate to one another. The excess of Lamech is at all costs to be avoided. His malign symmetry is to be replaced by the benign symmetry of the law of talion: an eye for an eye and a tooth for a tooth. This law is sometimes represented as a vengeful law, yet in reality it is the opposite. It forbids the vengefulness of Lamech in which a death is claimed for a blow, seventy-seven deaths for a single death. The symmetry of it is at once apparent. It establishes in real life what the law of reflection expresses in the Unconscious: if Cain knocks out Abel's tooth, then Abel may knock out Cain's tooth.

Situations which conform to the law of talion – in which 'tit' is returned for 'tat' – are situations which satisfy equally the demands of asymmetric logic – what is actually the case: and of symmetric logic – what the Unconscious believes to be the case. Since they fulfil both 'modes' of logic, we may adopt Matte Blanco's terminology and call such situations 'bi-modal'. What Consciousness perceives, and what the Unconscious believes, are in tune. The demands of both symmetric and asymmetric logic are therefore met. In the Law of Moses, this is the will of God, or in the terms adopted here, in this there is the key to harmony both among the many, and between the many and the One. In such situations the many express the symmetry of the One. The individual one does not strive to become the One, as Adam, Cain and Lamech did. Nor do differences between the many affront the symmetry beloved by the One. These laws express the theme of 'justice'.

Talion requires in particular that each individual in principle identifies him- or herself with each other individual. Lamech saw himself as infinitely important. Therefore he saw any assault on himself as an infinite assault deserving infinite reprisal. In the Covenant community no individual has greater value than another. A wound done to me is balanced by a similar wound returned, because my covenant brother is my equal. This mutuality is itself founded on symmetric logic through the modality of symbolism: I am an Israelite, my brother is an Israelite, therefore my brother and I are one. It extends explicitly, even beyond the covenant community, to the stranger: the symmetric logic of this extension is expressed in Exodus 22:21: 'You shall not wrong a stranger or oppress him, for you were strangers in the land of Egypt.' Therefore, you and the stranger are one.

Mutuality, bi-modality, will be explored further hereafter. The concept underlies the entire plan of God for the blessing on all humankind, as the Bible portrays it. For the moment we return to the biblical narrative.

While Moses is up the mountain the people take part in what sounds like an idolatrous orgy, returning presumably to the manifold gods of Egypt and falling into the Charybdis of ecstatic emotion, in which any passing feeling is regarded as infinite. The opposite end of a diabola is apparent when, after forty years wandering in the wilderness, they enter the Promised Land. Under a new leader, Joshua, ruthless extermination of the native peoples is carried out. With an excessive zeal for the God who has chosen them, they interpret his choice as a blessing solely upon the chosen – the Scylla of exclusivity.

Space forbids that we should follow the subsequent history during which Israel became a monarchy. The prophets emerged as particularly the preservers of the tradition of Israel's divine destiny. In transcendental experiences they perceived their calls from God and his choice of them. These calls in dreams and visions, through inner voices and by means, very often, of a play on words, show all the marks of an unfolding of the unrepressed Unconscious. The task of the prophet was again and again to recall Israel to its destiny as the chosen people, to regain the middle line between aggrandisement (Scylla) and absorption (Charybdis). For example, we find Isaiah hearing that 'it is too light a thing that you should be my servant to raise up the tribes of Jacob – I will give you as a light to the nations', (49:6). God's choice of one nation was made in order to bless all nations.

In the prophetic vocabulary there emerges the phrase 'a day of the Lord'. This will be a day when the righteous are vindicated, the oppressors overthrown – whether within Israel or beyond – and, within history, justice will be upheld. It will be a time when the covenant demands of mutual justice within the community are maintained: a time when Israel does not strive for its own existence by military might but 'trusts in the Lord': a time when, on the other hand, it does not lose itself among its neighbours and worship a variety of 'foreign' gods.

The centuries passed and Israel was taken captive in Babylon. Few signs remained of the promised glory. When the Persian empire arose, there was a return, but Israel became merely a province of successive empires – Persian, Greek, Greek-Syrian and, at last, Roman. The hope for a day of the Lord thereupon begins to expand: no longer will it be a political event within history, it becomes the ending of history and the emergence of a whole new creation in which the chosen will be heirs of a supernatural kingdom. At this time the righteous dead will rise and receive their reward and, along with the faithful who are left alive, they will enter the celestial banquet of rejoicing.

It was in this last context of ideas that the Christian era began. The next chapter will discuss that. The biblical history thus far needs to be summarised in the terms in which we are examining it. From the mystics we concluded in the last chapter that the Unconscious bestows a sense of cosmic unity and love. The myth of creation may be seen as expressing that, for it stands apparently in opposition to any account of the Unconscious that would make it indifferent to the asymmetric particularities of conscious life. In the history of Israel, as it was later recorded, we find two major and often divergent themes: the theme of choice, of relationship between the One and the one chosen from the many, and the theme of justice, the expression of symmetry and equality between the many. Only if choice is seen as a strategy towards justice can the two be reconciled.

Yet the two themes require each other. Choice without justice is arbitrary and leads to the individual – a person or a nation – seeing its own interest as absolute. Justice without choice is severed from its own source in symmetry, for the very impulse towards justice, which opposes the impulse to a narrow self-interest, comes from the mutuality that the symmetry of the One imposes.

The biblical history is the history of God's dealing with his people as Israel perceived it. The claim of Jewish and Christian faith is that that history reveals the true God. In earlier chapters, I have argued that the very notion of God is rooted in transcendental experience and is delineated in the writings of the mystics. The sense of cosmic unity is found in these to be close to the Unconscious. As this sense unfolds into consciousness we may see it as expressed in precisely the two themes of the biblical history which have been discussed. In choice – the ultimate is engaged with the particular, and in justice – in the sense that the ultimate is expressed in the mutuality of the particulars.

It may be objected that every nation is disposed to see itself in some way as 'chosen': why then attend so specifically to Israel? One can only respond that one does not choose one's own history and the biblical history is, for Jews and Christians, simply there. If other histories present a similar pattern, that is an argument for the validity of the pattern. On the individual level Thomas Traherne offered a remarkable insight:

> You never Enjoy the World aright, till the Sea itself floweth in your Veins, till you are Clothed with the Heavens, and Crowned with the Stars: and perceiv your self to be the Sole Heir of the whole world: [which is choice] and more than so, becaus Men are in it who are evry one Sole Heirs as well as you [which is mutuality and hence the root of justice].[9]

The paradox of the Sole Heir sums up the interplay between intimacy with God and mutuality with others. The paradox suggests that every particular history, driven by the symmetry of the Unconscious, may open a similar insight.

In discussing the biblical history I have used the term 'the One' to refer to God, to emphasise that I refer to that aspect of God I have called 'the Unconscious of God', an aspect discussed in symmetric logic. What then of the Consciousness of God in the history of Israel? Are there specific historical events in which God has acted and which therefore demand asymmetric assertions about him? These would provide evidence of the 'real existence' of another aspect of God, to which I have given the title 'the Consciousness of God'. Certainly the prophets – and others – believed in such a god and they spoke of a god who was 'a being', as well as 'Being-itself'. They believed in a God who might remember or forget, who might choose to intervene either in punishment or in restoration. Approached in the rational spirit of our own age, however, it would be hard to use the evidence of the biblical history to prove beyond reasonable doubt that a god of this kind exists. What we do find is the Unconscious unfolding in the Consciousness of Israel: this unfolding provides, on the one hand, a sense of intimacy with God (which makes Israel believe it is chosen), and, on the other hand, the understanding and desire for talionic justice (which is an unfolding of the symmetry of the One into a desire for harmony among the many).

We find, furthermore that, just as the creation stories mythically transmitted a certain understanding of God and the world, so too the distant past history operated mythically to disseminate an understanding of God's choice and of his justice. Particularly is this true of the crossing of the Red Sea, the making of the Covenant and the gift of the Promised Land. These events were culticly repeated year after year in the Passover, New Year and other Festivals. Through this repetition each successive generation identified itself with the generation that had first experienced them. They crossed the Red Sea again, heard the first reading of the Law, committed themselves anew to the keeping of the Covenant and took possession of the Promised Land. Furthermore, every sabbath day, Israel identified itself with God by sharing the sabbath rest of the seventh day of creation.

Cultic repetition of story is an ancient theme first found in Mircea Eliade's 'primordial humanity'; we will find it recurring in Christian history as the means by which the Unconscious unfolds through the medium of myth, in the fifth modality of Chapter 4. Within the pages of Scripture, we see history turning into myth. Stories about the action of a divine being are not for long treated as historical records, but as myths to be re-enacted, so as to experience in present time the eternal choice of God.

If Christian faith today finds meaning in the history of Israel it should not be as a source of evidence for the interventions of a divine being. On the contrary, it is the history of the unfolding of the Unconscious into Consciousness, an unfolding that delivers the two themes of this chapter: intimacy with the One, and symmetry between the many to express the symmetry of the One. If there is a Consciousness of God to be found here, it is not the consciousness of a separate divine being: it is human consciousness of this intimacy and justice.

9   Christ and the End

Christ is seen by Christians as fulfilling God's Old Testament purposes. What happened in Christ's life we cannot know. It was understood by the early Church as fulfilling those promises. This understanding was at first dominated by the expectation of the imminent End of the world. When this did not come, the story of Christ was translated into myth.

PROPHECY AND APOCALYPTIC

The last chapter explored the unfolding of the Unconscious in the history of Israel and began to give some clue to the nature of the Consciousness of God. This clue was mainly apparent in human consciousness – in the sense of choice and of justice. Israel believed itself chosen by God to bring blessing to the world. In terms of 'the One and the Many', this is a belief that one has been chosen from the many, to offer the hope of reconciling the many and the One.

'A day of the Lord' was a day in the prophetic vocabulary when God would reveal himself in the establishing of justice and in affirming his choice of Israel. These 'days' were expected to take place within the flow of history. The destruction of the Assyrian army by plague which ended the siege of Jerusalem was one such day.[1] Another, a day of judgement on Israel, fell when the leaders of the nation were taken captive to Babylon: and there was a day of restoration when the exiles returned. As Israel subsequently sank into political insignificance, expectation of such historical 'days' perhaps seemed less and less believable, though some, like the Maccabees, still hoped for them. Instead, a longing for a trans-historical day developed, a day in which the whole order of the world would be overturned as history ended and a new age of supernatural splendour dawned. These hopes began to be expressed in writings which are generally classified as 'apocalyptic': they speak of a revelation of God more universal and complete than any historical event could encompass.

Apocalyptic in Israel developed as prophecy declined, although some overlap may be discerned. Though new, it drew upon a much older stock of ideas. The Semitic nations of the whole region had for millennia perceived time as a succession of ages which would end in a supernatural restoration of the beginning. Such ideas were common to most of the religions of humankind and may be traced back to the primordial humanity about which Eliade wrote. The Great Time of the beginning would return in a Great Time at the End.

In Jewish apocalyptic there were suggestions that the world would pass through a week of ages and the seventh age would be an age of sabbath rest with God. It would be an age in which the righteous dead rose again and shared, with those who survived the destruction of the current order, in a banquet of everlasting rejoicing with God. Nationalism, doubtless, intruded into this vision at times and, for some, it may have been simply a justification of the faithful remnant of Israel. Nevertheless, it was a vision of the purification and restoration of the whole world. Potentially at least, even though much destruction might first take place, it could still express something of the universalist hope that all things might be reconciled in the age to come.

The resurrection of the dead was a distinctive feature of Jewish apocalyptic and one with momentous consequences. At the End individuals rose to rejoice with God. The End therefore did not bring about a return of the undifferentiated chaos before creation. In contrast, there is a popular Hindu image of death and the End as like a return of streams to the one universal Ocean of Being, in which all are swallowed up. This image is of the One reabsorbing the Many. The resurrection of the dead, however, expresses the continuance of the Many in harmony with the One. The consequences of this contrast for Christianity were momentous.

THE FULFILMENT OF PROPHECY

It was in an apocalyptic context of ideas that the decisive event for Christian faith took place – the coming of Christ.

If we ask what happened, we find ourselves in the midst of an immense scholarly debate, 'the quest for the historical Jesus'. It is a debate that furnishes few clear answers. If modern scholarship is agreed about anything, it is that even the Gospels are not biographies, but profoundly theological works. Our historical knowledge of Jesus comes almost wholly through the writings of his early disciples and they rapidly enwrapped what had happened in theological interpretations. Their purpose was not to satisfy the modern curiosity for accurate detail, but to present Jesus as the Lord and Saviour, the one who fulfilled all the promises made by God to Israel.

There is scarcely a detail of the New Testament records which can be claimed as quite certainly historically accurate. It does, however, seem probable that within a very few years of his death, and possibly even before it, the disciples of Jesus began to see in him the fulfilment of Old Testament promise. There was a belief, expressed in the last words of the prophet Malachi, that Elijah would come again just before the End. Though Jesus himself may have applied these words to John the Baptist (Mark 9:13), others applied them to him (Mark 8:28) and in the post-Resurrection discussion on the road to Emmaus he is again called a great prophet (Luke 24:19). In the Transfiguration vision he is seen in the company of Elijah and Moses apparently as, at least, a first among equals, inheriting thereby the mantles of both prophecy and law.

Jesus was seen as inheriting, also, the mantle of the kingship of Israel. The royal line of David had been promised an everlasting reign over Israel. St Matthew, in his opening genealogy, emphasised the descent of Jesus from David, presumably to assert this claim. Kings were anointed in Scripture as a sign of God's choice and Jesus is known as the Christ, the anointed one, in every surviving record. Some of his followers are recorded as intending to make him king, and it seems to have been a claim of which Pontius Pilate, too, was aware. As king, Jesus was seen to inherit uniquely the role of the chosen one.

In contrast to the more nationalistic spirit of St Matthew, St Luke begins his genealogy of Jesus from Adam and thus appears to emphasise the universal aspect of Jesus: the one who will bring God's blessing to all nations, a thought taken up by Simeon, the old man in the Temple who addressed Jesus as 'a light to lighten the Gentiles'.[2]

If Jesus was seen as inheriting the roles of law-giver (Moses), prophet (Elijah) and king (David), yet he was addressed as Rabbi or teacher, one who expounded the law and interpreted the stories of Israel. His teaching, as preserved, is predominantly about the kingdom of God, which was to be brought about by the End. The kingdom of which he spoke was very near, already among his disciples, and about to come suddenly upon the world. Among its attributes was the reversal of power and status, so that the mighty were to be cast down, the lowly raised up. In the kingdom the injustice and inequality of the current age would be redressed and a true justice established.

Among the prophecies most linked with Jesus by his disciples were those of Isaiah which spoke of redemption through the suffering of a just 'servant of God'.[3] Who this servant was originally has been much debated and perhaps most probable is the view that it described no particular historical figure, but, rather, the true role of Israel, to undergo suffering vicariously for the sins of the world.

Jesus was described also as a Son of God, though this may mean little more than a good servant of God. The title 'Son of Man' is more significant. It is an ambiguous phrase which might merely mean 'a man', and may have been used by Jesus as a periphrasis for 'I'. Yet it was also applied, in a unique sense, to the one who was to be the agent of God in bringing about the End, the second Adam, a supernatural figure first encountered in the book of Daniel.

THE EXPECTED END

In all these roles we notice various echoes of the master theme of Israel's existence: the choice of God for the bringing of universal blessing through a justice which would redress the injustices of history. The distinctive turn that these themes took in Jesus is largely explicable by the background of apocalyptic. What he himself believed is highly disputable, but it is certain that his disciples were convinced that the End of the world would follow closely after his death. Evidence was provided by the Spirit: the ecstatic phenomena, particularly speaking with tongues, which were experienced in the early church, fulfilled the prediction of an outpouring of the Spirit 'on all flesh'. By far the most important sign, however, was the resurrection of Jesus from the dead, for this was seen as the beginning of a general resurrection at the End. St Paul later called it the first-fruits[4] of this, and when St Matthew wrote his Gospel he included a belief that others had risen at the moment of Christ's death.[5]

I do not propose to discuss at this point whether Jesus' resurrection was 'a real event'. To understand the early church's theologising of Christ, we have to return to the question of eschatology. There is much to support the view that Jesus believed the end of the world was very near and quite possibly that it was his role to bring that end about through his sacrificial death. As the Gospels record it, his own teaching about the End stressed the urgency of repentance, for only those who repented would enter the kingdom. In his life-time it is asserted that disciples were sent out to proclaim its imminence and immediately after his death the apostles are described as going out to all nations to deliver the same message.

Knowledge of the first years of the church paradoxically comes to us from the later books of the New Testament. The earliest books are the first letters of St Paul which tell us much of his own time, but very little about the years before it. Thus the Acts of the Apostles, written in AD 80–90 provides almost our only knowledge of the events following Jesus' Resurrection up to, say, AD 50. On the other hand, St Paul's first letters dating from AD 50–60 give us reliable information about the church at that date. Since the author of the Acts was almost certainly influenced by Paul, any effort to reconstruct a pre-Pauline history or theology is fraught with controversy.

Despite these difficulties it is possible to argue with reasonable confidence that opinion about 'the End' passed through two stages. The first of these stressed its immediacy: it was expected in the lifetime of Jesus' first disciples. Awkward references to this remain in the Gospels, written when the passage of time had already disproved such a belief. The same belief is found in the earlier letters of Paul. The Gospel message in this stage was of great simplicity. The world was about to end in a destruction by fire more total even that that which occurred by flood in the time of Noah. Those who repented would be saved from it. Repentance was expressed by baptism in the name of Jesus; those who trusted in his lordship over the age to come would be recognised and delivered. Baptism might be compared with the blood on the lintel of the door which preserved Hebrew families from the loss of the their first-born in the last plague in Egypt. It marked out those who would escape destruction. This belief inspired St Paul in his determination to take the Gospel to the ends of the earth, gathering in those to be saved from the approaching wrath. Passionately he believed that the Gospel was for Gentile as well as for Jew, salvation and the consequent blessing was potentially universal. This indeed was the mystery laid up from the foundation of the world, but only revealed 'in our time'. He, and those like him who spread the good news, were agents of reconciliation between God and humankind because the End of the world was near. It might come the next day, or the next year, certainly in the next few years. The message was therefore of great urgency. Although the End would bring an end to history, it was an event within history, with all the reality that a nuclear catastrophe might have in our own times. The ancient myth of the End had become imminent fact.

THE END DELAYED

The End did not come, however, and in the letters attributed to St Paul a gradual development may be traced to take account of that awkward fact. Even in the relatively early letter to the Romans St Paul began to conceive of a history yet to be unfolded before the End came. The success of the Gentile mission was to bring the Jews to their senses and to shame them into accepting that Christ was the fulfilment of biblical promise. Their unfaithfulness was part of the plan of God to open salvation to all nations and thereby fulfil the original aim of a universal blessing. Christ alone had inherited the chosen role of Israel, but, through the spread of the Gospel, people of all nations were claiming adoption into the same sonship of God. The ruling powers of the world opposed this process, but eventually every enemy would be overcome. Finally, as St Paul put it in the first letter to the Corinthians, 'the dead will rise and share in the kingdom in which all is subject to Christ, who then himself will also be made subject, and thus God will be all in all'.[6]

In Ephesians, St Paul (or a later disciple of his – the authorship is debatable) wrote with still greater clarity of God's secret purpose which would be put into effect when the time was ripe.[7] This secret purpose was that the universe, 'everything in heaven and on earth, might be brought into a unity in Christ'.

It is clear that the End had receded at least into the middle distance, so to speak. With this recession everything else changed as well. Baptism had been a passport to immediate salvation from a literal destruction: it became the beginning of a process of transformation of the individual into the likeness of Christ. The Spirit had been an ecstatic sign of the End: instead it became the agent of this transformation. Whereas speaking with tongues had been a chief mark of its activity, growth in faith, hope and, above all, love became the main proof of the Spirit's presence.

The nature of the Christian's relationship to Christ changed also. Christ had been the one taken up into heaven who would return as the agent of the End: one who was therefore temporarily absent. Instead he became an indwelling presence: if the believer was 'in Christ' then Christ was also 'in' the believer. St Paul goes so far as to speak of his true life as being not his own, but as Christ's within him. A mere enlistment in the company of those who would escape destruction had changed into a personal experience of the indwelling of the saving Lord.

The Resurrection of Christ became less important as a sign of the imminent End, more important as evidence for the hope that, after death, the faithful Christian would share in the ultimate triumph of God. The death of Christ had, at first, been an historical event which was probably seen as 'triggering off' the beginning of the End. It became an event in which, in baptism, the individual participated: St Paul wrote, 'in baptism all die with Christ so that they may share in his resurrection'. At some point, resurrection, as well as death, became an event which the Christian had already, in some sense or to some degree, experienced. To this point I shall return shortly.

The End itself changed from a sudden destruction to the fruit of a long process, the process by which Christ would become 'all in all'. In subsequent generations, if not immediately, this was expected to come through the growth of the church and the conversion of all humankind – or, at least, of that part of it which was not irredeemably evil. The enemies of God were not to be overcome by a sudden act of divine power and wrath, but through the crucifixion of Christ, whose suffering had mysteriously defeated the powers of evil.

This was a development of the line of thought expressed in the Servant Songs of Isaiah: the purpose of God was to be brought about by the submission of the sacrificial victim, not by mere force alone.

The secret purpose of God that was revealed in Christ and which would be accomplished fully at the End included, therefore, the reversal of power – the weak would become strong, the victims the conquerors. It also included the making of peace between opposites, Jew and Gentile, male and female, slave and free. All these were aspects of the state in which Christ was to be all in all.

THE BLESSING OF PEACE

Belief in an imminent End in which most of creation would be destroyed was hardly a worthy expression of the belief in universal blessing, of the bringing of the many into unity with the one. On the contrary, it seemed to express God's impatience with his creatures in much the same way as had the story of the Flood. St Paul's later eschatology recovered the universal vision: God would be all in all. The many would return to the one. Resurrection of the individual, however, gave this vision that distinctive feature which we have already noted. The many would not be absorbed back into the one, but would preserve their individuality. The one would indwell the many, and the many would *continue to be* in the One.

This process is the making of peace. In the biblical and Jewish tradition peace is not mere rest, nor does it come about through ignoring the wrongs of the past. It is the establishment of genuine justice. All accounts are settled, and settled universally. What talion established over one matter between two parties, universal peace would establish over every matter between all parties. Included in this reconciliation is the relationship between God and humanity.

We must now consider this reconciliation in the light of bi-logic. Talion took an asymmetry – *A has injured B* – and made it symmetrical, by a reciprocal act – *B has injured A*. I have described the resulting state as 'bi-modal', since it is both symmetrical and, also, preserves the factual truth only describable through asymmetrical perception. Talion brought the perceived facts of conscious awareness into line with the symmetric working of the Unconscious. In a state of peace which is both just and universal every individual has justice: a balance between what has been done to each is struck with what each has done. Talion achieves this in a perspective that sees only two parties. The law of rotation achieves this between three, for if A has injured B and B has injured C, then if C injures A, a symmetric harmony is achieved. Something of this sort is expressed in the parable of the Master and his Two servants.[8] The Master forgives the first servant a large debt. The servant goes away and demands repayment of a small debt from the second servant, and demands it with violence. The Master, informed of this, then rescinds his forgiveness and the first servant is cast into prison.

In the teaching of Christ, the means by which peace is to be achieved is not retaliation, but forgiveness. The Lord's prayer does not ask, 'Repay our debts, as we repay those who are indebted to us'; instead, it runs: 'Forgive us our trespasses, as we forgive those who have trespassed against us.' This is a symmetric reversal of retaliation, since instead each is to focus not on *What they owe me*, but on *What I have done to them*. Each is to forgive the other's debt, knowing that they themselves have debts to yet others, and particularly to God. The end result is to be a universal bi-modality, where the forgiveness each bestows is matched by the forgiveness each receives, where therefore the reality perceived by consciousness is in a symmetry, agreeable to the Unconscious. Such is the Christian solution to the problem of the one and the many.

FACTS AND FAITH

What then have we found of the Consciousness of God in the New Testament account of Jesus? The sense of cosmic unity found by the mystics in the Unconscious unfolds into a drive for justice. Hints of how creation might express this unity, through justice, are provided by the vision of the End found in St Paul's mature thinking. The manner in which choice and justice might be reconciled in an ultimate peace is clarified. In the Consciousness of the body of believers there has been a development and that development is an unfolding of the Unconscious. But if we had hoped to find evidence in the story of Jesus for the action of a divine, supreme being, we will be disappointed. If we found such, then we might well identify it as the Consciousness of God. Instead we have found the eternal Unconscious unfolding in the Consciousness of the emerging church.

I have asserted that as we approach the New Testament in the spirit of historical inquiry we can find no provable trace of the action of a supreme being. That needs further discussion for many believers will point to the miracles of Jesus and, above all, to his resurrection, as evidence of just such an action. But to use these as evidence is a circular argument: for if the New Testament records are approached by historical inquiry, then, as in any other such inquiry into distant times, we can only produce probabilities for the factuality of any particular event. If one already believes there is a divine actor in human affairs, then it may be plausible to believe that he raised Jesus from the dead. If one does not, then any explanation of why the disciples believed Jesus to have risen is more plausible than to believe that he actually rose. Historical inquiry is inevitably trapped in its own presuppositions as to what sort of things happen in the world. An alleged miracle, far distant from one in time, will never be taken as historical evidence for anything in which one was not already disposed to believe.

Historical inquiry is the means by which facts about the past are established. It is conducted principally in the sphere of asymmetric logic. The attempt to apply this logic to the events described in the New Testament simply reveals the presuppositions with which one has begun the inquiry. Faith is therefore ill-advised to appeal to the resurrection as a factual proof of its validity. Scholarly New Testament criticism in the last two centuries has wholly embraced the methods of historical inquiry through literary criticism and its consequences for the faith of many have therefore been devastating. As has already been observed, nearly every detail of the Scriptures has been made questionable. Those who have suffered most from this are those who have believed most firmly that the facts matter.

Some have adopted biblical literalism as a refuge: what is in the Bible is true because the Bible is given by God as, among other things, an infallible record of the past. The Bible, thus treated, is regarded as a source of factual information of guaranteed accuracy, superior to what other methods of inquiry might establish. I regard such a belief as pure superstition and do not propose to debate with it. Many others, not willing to pervert their intellect in such a way, have pursued scholarly criticism in the hope of finding some certain residue of fact. This, the quest for the historical Jesus, has, however, produced no certain agreed results. Instead of certainties, this approach leaves those who put their faith in Scripture as a revelation of God with nothing but a mass of scholarly uncertainties.

There is a way out of this situation, which depends upon neither adopting the false rock of fundamentalism nor sinking into the whirlpool of scholarly uncertainties. It is the recognition that the story of Christ, like the stories of creation and the fall, is a myth. Myths are not judged by facts, but instead create the presuppositions by which factuality is determined. Active in transitional space, they are beyond the criterion of reality or falsity. They are lodged in the depths of the mind – or they are not. They are not put there by historical inquiry or by any other rational procedure, though these may create or remove obstacles to their influence.

To claim that the Resurrection is a fact is to subject it to the rightful demands of historical inquiry, to the shifting sands of scholarly opinion. To allow that it is the central episode of a myth is to remove it from this sphere entirely. For those to whom the myth is embedded in the soul, questions of fact need not be of interest. As I once heard a Greek Orthodox theologian say (I cannot recall her name): 'We do not ask whether or not the resurrection happened, it is the horizon within which we live.'[9] It is this view that I shall pursue in the next chapter, to examine whether it is an adequate basis for Christian faith. I turn then to the defence of the claim that Christian faith depends not upon facts but upon the myth of Christ.

10 The Myth of Christ

Christians speak of God becoming incarnate in Christ. This sounds like a divine intervention in history. What we find, instead, is the unfolding of the Unconscious in the myth that arose from the memories of Christ. As a figure in myth, Christ came to be seen as eternal, ubiquitous, symbolic and paradoxical. What really happened is unknown, and, in reality, unimportant. Faith is not about historical facts, but about embedding myth in deep levels of the mind.

CHRIST AND THE GREAT TIME

For the sake of clarity, though at the risk of tediousness, I shall recapitulate the discussion of the last chapter.

There are virtually no certain facts about the life of Christ and undoubtedly none can be established which would prove the claims about him subsequently made by the church.[1]

It is probable, though nothing can be held to be certain, that in, let us say, the first twenty years of the church's history, an apocalyptic view of Christ prevailed. The last days of history had arrived and the End of the World was approaching. The death of Christ in some way fulfilled the destiny of Israel and his Resurrection was the proof that this was so. God, conceived as a supreme being, was about to intervene in the course of history. He, or the Risen Christ as his agent, was about to return in judgement and after the destruction of the known world, would reign in glory in a new age with the saints, those who had acknowledged his lordship through repentance and baptism. Faith was belief in this and believers were faithfully to cling to it through whatever tribulations might remain until the End.

In this view, God was about to act in history. The Resurrection was a fact which proved it. The End was an imminent event.

But the End did not come and the realisation began to dawn that somehow this apocalyptic vision was not right. Christianity might have died forthwith, as, many centuries later, did the Catholic Apostolic church[2] which revived the belief in a very near end. Christianity did not die, but instead, as far as we know largely through the influence of St Paul, it transformed itself into a religion equipped with an understanding of history, and history continued under the same temporal conditions as before.

The End receded and finally, on the basis of St Paul's understanding, though perhaps not fully in his own thinking, it returned to the sphere of myth. It receded to a remote future in which Christ was to be all in all, not through the violence of an apocalyptic descent from heaven, but through conversion and the growth of the church. Officially in the teaching of the church belief that the End was to come in history, and might come at any time, remained. In practice, except in marginal sects, the church has been content to live with a distant prospect of the End. The sense of urgency which the End once inspired was replaced by the urgency inspired by mortality – no one could know the moment of their own death. The Judgement that mattered was the one that followed upon individual death and decided eternal destiny; the relationship between it and 'the Last Judgement' at the end of history was unclear. The Christian hope changed from hope that the End was near, to hope for a good death, a merciful judgement, and life with God in heaven above.

The Resurrection was no longer the proof that the End was near, for the End had returned to the sphere of myth. The Resurrection was no longer needed as a fact therefore, but became part of a story re-enacted in the life of the believer. The story goes back to the beginning: each human being shares personally in the Fall of Adam and shares his death penalty.[3] Faith, however, adds a new identification, with Christ, the second Adam, and the believer shares in his Resurrection. Thus St Paul wrote, 'As in Adam all die, so also in Christ shall all be made alive'.[4] In the likeness of Adam, the first man, the man of dust[5], all have sinned and suffer the penalty of death. In the likeness of Christ, the second man, the man from heaven, the saved shall rise.

> The man made of dust is the pattern of all who are made of dust, and the heavenly man is the pattern of all the heavenly. As we have worn the likeness of the man made of dust, so we shall wear the likeness of the heavenly man.[6]

The life of a believer is to be interpreted as partaking, first in the Great Time at the beginning, but then also and more so, in a new Great Time, the story of Christ, so that finally he or she may participate in the general Resurrection in the Great Time at the End.

Participation in Christ's death and Resurrection was for St Paul especially connected with baptism. He wrote:

Have you forgotten that when we were baptised into union with Christ Jesus we were baptised into his death? By that baptism into his death we were buried with him, in order that, as Christ was raised from the dead by the glorious power of the Father, so also we might set out on a new life.[7]

Baptism was participation in the death of Christ and the new life it brought was participation in his Resurrection. It is true that there is something a little provisional about Resurrection, for in one sense it is still to come – when the last trump shall sound. However, the new life of Christians is life 'in Christ' and that can only mean in his risen life. Furthermore, if Christians are in Christ then Christ is in Christians, and St Paul wrote of his own life as not his own, but Christ's within him.[8] The symmetric logic of 'Christ in the Christian' and 'the Christian in Christ' should be noted, a perfect instance of the law of reflection. The modalities, described above in Chapter 4, at once appear as well.

CHRIST AND THE MODALITIES

Eternity

Eternity is expressed by the abolition of time as the present participates in the past. In baptism the candidate takes part in a past event. The figure of Christ, whom the first disciples knew as a man, takes on transcendent dimensions. In St John's Gospel the words 'Before Abraham was, I am',[9] are put into his lips, an assertion without parallel in the other Gospels. In the prologue of St John, Christ's pre-existence is stretched back to before creation, 'In the beginning was the Word.'[10] Furthermore, as expectation of an imminent return recedes, his sitting at the right hand of the father is not a temporary session in the brief interlude before his return. It becomes an ever-lasting co-presence with God: as the letter to the Hebrews puts it, Christ the same, yesterday and today and for ever.[11] Or again in the Apocalypse, Christ is 'Alpha and Omega, the beginning and the end.'[12] Jesus has become timeless.

Infinity

St Luke's and St Matthew's accounts of the Ascension retain the belief in an imminent End. Jesus is transported bodily into a physically located heaven from which he would soon bodily return. The Spirit of God might be poured upon the Apostles, but it came from an absent Jesus, as an interim pledge of the decisive intervention

soon to come While these accounts post-date most or all of the
Pauline letters, they reflect a more primitive understanding. For St
Paul, Christ, like the Spirit, is an indwelling presence in the Christian
and his physical body (Adam's body of dust) is transmuted into life-
giving Spirit. It thereby becomes placeless, for it may be anywhere.
Christ in St Paul is omnipresent: he indwells the Christian wherever
the Christian may be. It becomes something of a problem to distinguish this indwelling Christ from the Spirit of God. When the body
of Christ is spoken of, it refers to the company of believers, or to the
bread of the Eucharist, not to a physical body located above the skies.
In St Paul the physical finitude of Jesus is lost in the ubiquity of God.
This is the modality of infinity.

Symbolism

The telling of the story itself was, from the first days, impossible
without symbolism, for almost every incident in the life of Christ was
seen as the fulfilling of Scripture, which thereby became a catalogue
of symbols – Moses, Elijah and David, as discussed above, were
symbolically related to Jesus. He was also bread, wine, light, life, the
sacrificial Lamb, the giver of rebirth, and in the title of 'Lord', previ-
ously reserved for the Almighty, he became implicitly a symbol of
God.

Symbolism, in the powerful form of identification of oneself with
another, is evident in the identification of the Christian with Christ.
To be a Christian at all is to be 'in Christ'. His crucifixion came to
be seen as the Christian's own death, and his Resurrection as the
Christian's passing through death. Christ's story became the story of
the Christian's life – as is expressed very clearly in the modern
Roman Catholic Eucharist:

> By his birth we are reborn,
> in his suffering we are freed from sin.
> By his rising from the dead we rise to everlasting life.
> In his return to you in glory
> we enter into your heavenly kingdom.[13]

Paradox

Paradox appears in many aspects in the relationship of Christ and
Christian. Perhaps, at the beginning, it was enough to believe that in
Jesus the promises and predictions of the Old Testament were
fulfilled; and that therefore God was about to act. All that was
needed was repentance in preparation for this and membership of the

body of believers. But once identification between the Holy Christ and the sinful Christian became explicit, paradoxes multiplied. The Just one has died for the unjust so that they may be accounted just by God. The sinless one has been made sin so that sin may be overcome. The infinite eternal Lord, the immortal Son of God, has undergone death to defeat death. Christians who are heirs to the world and in whom the Lord of creation dwells are yet the rubbish and off-scourings of creation. Finally, those who become Christians are not so much those who choose to repent, but those who have been chosen from the foundation of the world.[14]

Story

The fifth modality, as often elsewhere, is dependent upon the other four: their presence disposes us to infer its presence also, and indeed I have already claimed that the Resurrection was changing: it had been an alleged fact which proved the nearness of the End, it was becoming a myth in which the believer participated across the bounds of time and space. The implication is that the death and Resurrection are not required by faith to be factual events. This is a matter of passionate current controversy and I shall return to it shortly.

THE TRANSFORMING CHRIST

Baptism was not administered – or perhaps conceivable – without a turning away from sin and the creating of a new mind and heart. The baptism of John the Baptist in the synoptic Gospels required a new standard of outward behaviour. Repentance was required, a turning away from ill-doing. Tax-collectors were told not to exact more than they should and soldiers not to bully or blackmail.[15] Only thus would they escape the wrath to come. These details are found only in St Luke, who is expanding a passage of St Mark. They may therefore be taken to express the author's understanding of repentance, as much as John the Baptist's. They are parallelled by such incidents involving Jesus as the repentance of the tax-collector Zacchaeus.[16] He redeemed himself by returning his ill-gotten exactions four-fold and that was all there was to it. This is something very different from the transformation of the heart and soul by the indwelling of the risen Christ.

The new relationship with God that St Paul described was far deeper and more complex than mere restraint from injustice. It was a covenant written on the hearts of believers,[17] as the prophets had foretold. Doubtless there were always some whose reception of the

Gospel was shallow (as in Jesus' parable of the Sower[18]). For those who remained faithful the Gospel brought deep change, change that would now be described as at unconscious as well as conscious levels. St Paul, for example, as a Pharisee, had believed that God required the precise keeping of the Jewish law. The effort to do so however had not brought him peace of mind, but ever deeper guilt. 'Who will deliver me from this body of death?',[19] he asked himself reflecting upon this period. At a deep level of the soul the law was reinforcing the message, 'You are wrong, guilty, condemned.' The Gospel brought to him a new message, 'You are reconciled to God, declared righteous through the death of Christ.' St Paul's Gospel was not a call to abandon outward wrongdoing, though certainly that was a consequence of it. First of all, however, it was a transformation of the unconscious depths of the soul, of which outward change was the expected fruit.

Our knowledge of the events of Jesus' life and of the earliest years of the church is very much a matter of speculation. The earliest Gospel, St Mark's, was written after many of St Paul's letters, possibly after all of them, and its author may very well have been influenced by Paul, or may even have known him. Nevertheless, with some confidence we can deduce that a belief in an imminent end of the world in which the repentant might be saved became a faith through which people articulated a relationship with God that would serve them for the natural term of life, without any End in immediate sight. The Gospel changed from a proclamation of the end, to a call for a transformation of the soul and spirit of humankind. A literal eschatology was replaced, therefore, in a broad sense of the word, by psychology. The simple assertion of a presumed fact, 'the End of the world' is near, was replaced by a story increasingly expressed through the modalities, and thus calculated to address the unconscious depths of the soul. The Gospel moved from the simplicities of the calendar, into transitional space. The Risen Christ was no longer above the clouds but in the third heaven to which St Paul was transported. 'Whether in the body or not I know not',[20] he said, but we may assume it was in the spirit. The Gospel thereby became a means of transforming the depths of the soul. The End, no longer an imminent historical reality, had become a vision and inspiration in the struggle for earthly justice. Christians, rather than awaiting a Noachian retribution, are engaged in the transformation of themselves and the world.

Baptism, as the means of entry to the redeemed community, was at first of the utmost importance. However, it could be performed only once in a life-time. As the story of Christ became a story in which the believer participated, more was needed. Christians no longer entered once into a brief time of waiting: they began to expect a life-time of transformation into the likeness of Christ. Thus the repeatable sacrament of the Eucharist gradually eclipsed in significance the once for all act of baptism. Whatever the Eucharist was in the beginning – and that is much disputed – it became in effect a weekly re-baptism, for the believer stepped out of ordinary time into the sacred time of the new sabbath and there re-enacted the story of Christ's death and Resurrection. St Paul's understanding of baptism had made it an expression of something very like the Great Time of Eliade's myths. The believer put on Christ, much as the hunter put on the persona of the Great Hunter of myth. The story by the acquisition of the modalities began to work as a myth, in transitional space, addressing unconscious disposition as well as outward behaviour. As the Eucharist gradually dominated Christian living in the centuries after St Paul, the mythological nature of the story was further emphasised, and the Eucharist was the predominant cultic expression of it.

The process was an inevitable one, if Christianity was to survive and to guide people in the search for God. Only a story expressed through the modalities can address the depths of the soul, since only such a story can engage with the Unconscious. There is, therefore, a legitimate comparison to be made between the Christian story and both Eliade's myths and Bettelheim's fairy stories. The manner of communication is essentially very similar, although in each case there are very large distinctions also to be made. As Jung wrote, 'Myth is the natural and indispensable intermediate stage between unconscious and conscious cognition'.[21] Only a mythical manner of communicating can guide the soul in search of God.

I shall turn aside from the main argument to note in passing some of these distinctions. In contrast to primordial myth, the Christian both becomes Christ and is also sharply aware of his or her difference from Christ. The identity with Christ is, in its fullness, something to be hoped for, when Christ will be all in all. Next, in primordial myth, the past and future Great Times are one and the same – there is an eternal *return*. Christian faith, as is often said, begins in a Garden (of Eden), but ends in a City (the heavenly Jerusalem). The future is different from the past, and this allows Christianity to have a view of history as progressive, rather than repetitive. This is echoed in the Eucharist, which is a kind of repetition of past events in the earthly Jerusalem, or, more accurately, a return to them, but it is also a participation in the heavenly banquet which is yet to come.

Bettelheim's fairy stories address specific fears and aspirations belonging to particular periods of child development. The Christian story addresses matters on a broader scale: the fear of death, the haunting sense of guilt, the threat of meaninglessness. It is an account of the nature of existence, of the movement, driven by love and justice, from the One to the many to the many-in-One. The Christian story is, therefore, involved in matters which are not outgrown as the fears of childhood may be. It embraces the whole of life, not transition from one stage to another. The Christian story is not a child's fairy story, even though the manner of communication, through the modalities, is distinctly similar.

THE RESURRECTION – MIRACLE OR MYTH?

I return now to the postponed question raised by the fifth modality – the equivalence in story of fantasy and reality. Detractors of Christianity have used the words 'myth' and 'fairy stories' as terms of abuse for its story. Against such, Christians have claimed that their story is true. More specifically, and in current debate, Christians have argued that the Resurrection really happened and that the historical evidence for it is good. It is often described as the fact upon which Christianity rests.

Returning to the main argument, we remember that, in the brief period of eschatological expectancy, the factual truth of the Resurrection was clearly of the greatest importance. If Christ had risen, then the end of the world was about to arrive in a literal and physical sense – for Resurrection was one of the chief signs of it. Once this belief became marginalised, the relationship between the believer and Christ's Resurrection was transformed. The Resurrection became rapidly – and remains today – not a proof of faith, but the object of faith. That is to say, it is no longer evidence supporting belief in the approaching End of the world, but rather it is itself a matter of faith.

There are some who claim that the Bible is the inerrant word of God, directly inspired by him as an incontrovertible record of fact. To such, the word of God is certain evidence of the facticity of the Resurrection. No purpose is served by wasting words in response to such an argument.

There are others who argue that the evidence of the four Gospels should be taken seriously as historical evidence. In response to this we must note that in two centuries of scholarly debate about the Gospels almost nothing has been established with factual certainty about the historical Jesus: there is almost no word of his teaching or particular incident in his life which has not plausibly been argued to be fictitious. Historical evidence must be assessed by honest historical investigation, and that can seldom produce more than probabilities. If such methods are applied to an event like the Resurrection, the argument becomes circular: for how can an event which we would normally describe as impossible ever be evaluated in terms of probability? Only, surely, if we are disposed to believe in its likelihood in advance; only if we think God does things like that. But we have no experience of him doing so: no one else appears to have been raised from the dead in like fashion, however meritorious their lives. It might be answered that no one else is the unique Son of God – however, if you ask why we think Jesus was the unique Son of God, it is because he rose from the dead (or at least that was why the first Christians gave him such a unique status). Circularity inevitably returns.

In a sense the very concept of Resurrection is self-contradictory, for if today a man who appeared clinically dead came back to life, it would be argued that, despite the clinical signs of death, he was never truly dead. What Christians claim of Christ is quite different from a survival of that kind: what is claimed is that he defeated the powers of death, descended to the place of the dead, and robbed the powers of evil of their prey.

It seems – to summarise much debate – that all arguments about the facts of the Resurrection fail to deliver what the Christian faith appears to need of them. It is precisely here that the fifth modality, so far from threatening Christian faith, actually comes to its rescue. We need to admit that as far as discursive reasoning and historical investigation go, we can establish nothing about the Resurrection, and we therefore must place the story of the Resurrection firmly in transitional space. As subject to the fifth modality, its factual truth or falsity is of no significance. It is not in that realm at all. Even to ask the question whether it happened or did not happen is to misconstrue the logic of its *modus operandi*. For the Christian the Resurrection occurs in the Great Time whose stories express, and indeed constitute, what is ultimately significant in a sense quite different from historical fact.

Since this is a point of such importance, it is well to remember where the fifth modality originally came from. In his analysis of disturbed people, Freud found that many problems arose from repressed conscious material to do with their sexual abuse as children. The question of 'false memory syndrome' is currently a vexed one, and professional opinion has changed many times as to whether in the majority of reported cases abuse has actually taken place. Freud's discovery was that it was not abuse in itself that left unconscious disturbance, but the memory of it. What were reported in analysis as memories, however, were not necessarily memories of real events. Possibly, in very many cases, they were memories of something feared to be real. The important matter for the analyst in either case was not what had happened, but rather the uncovered fantasy that purported to be a memory. It was not what had happened in itself that did the damage, it was the powerful story in the mind, whether or not it was based on fact.

Analogously, since we are thinking of the same deep level of the mind where unconscious and conscious interact, it is not the fact of the Resurrection that has saving power, but the story of it at work in the depths of the soul. To ask whether it happened is to ask the wrong question.

The frightened child is not reassured if he is told that giants do not exist. He wants to know whether they are nearby. Likewise, the Christian does not need to consider whether the Resurrection is an historical fact: he or she wants to know whether it is possible to partake of eternal life now.

CHRIST AND THE CONSCIOUSNESS OF GOD

In the Christ story (and through the Old Testament) the God of the mystics is expressed through the image of the eternal Father, Creator, etc. – through archetypal images. In the Christ story he is joined by an archetypal Son who takes on a human life, dies, rises and returns to glory. In the search for the Consciousness of God we are looking for some action in history which can be decisively attributed to God. The revelation of Christ might be such. But if we look at it, we find no factual certainty and, indeed, factual certainty is irrelevant to our mode of relating to the story. The most we can say with historical certainty is that a particular story emerged out of whatever happened in the events of Jesus' life. The mode of divine operation, therefore, is in changing human consciousness through stories emerging under powerful unconscious influence. As to whether some extraterrestrial power impelled certain events, such as the Resurrection, actually to take place, we simply have no means of knowing and the question remains an open one. Faith, despite what is often said, is not existentially involved in answering it.

The teaching of Christ expresses with greater clarity the two themes of choice and justice found in the Old Testament, themes which we have interpreted as the unfolding of the One into the many and the reconciling of the many with the One. A significant emphasis is put upon achieving justice, not through talion, but through forgiving and being forgiven. The Christian may well see in this teaching the Unconscious of God unfolding into the consciousness of the historical Jesus and traditional ways of thinking of the divinity of Christ may tempt one to see in him the Consciousness of God. Something like this seems compatible with the thinking of Friedrich Schleiermacher whose lectures in 1798[22] are often considered the beginning of modern theology. He argued that the divine nature of Jesus arose from the intensity of his awareness of God, which, I suppose, must imply that he incarnated the Consciousness of God itself.

If one followed this line of thought one might see the work of the Holy Spirit in the church as a further unfolding of the Consciousness of God. In the first years of Christianity charismatic phenomena, such as speaking in tongues, were evidence of the nearness of the End. St Paul, however, began to relate the presence of the Spirit more to love and unity. When a group of Christians were of one mind, then the Holy Spirit was active. Likewise, the Apostles are recorded as declaring, 'It seemed good to the Holy Spirit and to us',[23] in the Acts of the Apostles. We may claim that here is the presence of the Consciousness of God, for the Holy Spirit in such contexts has a clearly asymmetric way of thinking: in that case precise regulations were prescribed by the Spirit. Group analysis is a development of Freudian thinking in which a number of people explore themselves under the direction of a group analyst. The theory of group analysis has made much of 'the group mind', as though a trans-personal consciousness develops greater than the consciousness of each individual. One might speculate that a group acting appropriately under the inspiration of the myth of Christ might develop, in something of the same way, a group mind, which could be equated with the Consciousness of God. One might note the possibility of demonic spirits, for the group mind can be dysfunctional and diabolic under bad leadership, and we find St John urging his readers to test the spirits.[24] In this we might choose to see the Consciousness of the Devil!

As we look at the origins of Christianity historically we do not find evidence for the intervention of a divine being through miraculous events. What we find is an unfolding of the Unconscious, first, probably in the life of the man Jesus, but continuing among his followers. This unfolding soon shapes the memories of that life into mythical form and thus passes them on through the sacraments and stories of the church.

11   Christ and Doctrine

In the course of time rational reflection on the myth led to the formation of doctrine. The appearance of rationality is belied by the persistence of the modalities: where myth was replaced by reason, at once reason was beset by paradox which undermined it. The doctrines of the Trinity and Incarnation, particularly, are dominated by symmetric logic and become virtually expressions of its laws.

THE EUCHARIST AS RE-ENACTMENT

The Eucharist became the dominant expression of Christian faith and, as the centuries passed, it more clearly took on the character of a symbolic re-enactment of the Christian story. The purpose of the re-enactment was to identify the believer with Christ, the myth of Christ with the story of the believer's life. Repetition embedded the myth in the Unconscious, and so, too, did the manner in which it came to be celebrated. Poetic and rhetorical speech, art and, above all, music were used to appeal to unconscious levels of the mind.

The Eucharist is a repetition of certain events of the Last Supper, in which, on the night before he died, Jesus is recorded as having used bread and wine to explain the significance of his approaching death. As these acts were repeated by his disciples they took on a wider significance. They did not just explain his death, but they were seen by St Paul to proclaim his death as well. The bread and wine were not mere signs, for in eating them the believer received the body and blood of Christ. The breaking of the bread for distribution echoed the breaking of Christ's body on the Cross. The consumption of the bread and wine was the reception of Christ's risen life, a participation in his resurrection. Like baptism, the Eucharist, in a subsequently much disputed sense, therefore became a symbolic re-enactment of the decisive events of the story of Christ.

The symbolic re-enactment never took on the crude character of allegory, in which each act of the cultic officials represented a specific event of the story of Christ. Yet the sacrifice of Christ was offered again and believers were in some sense present at the original events.

But they were also in heaven and the saints were present at the liturgy, which was a foretaste of the heavenly banquet at the end of time. Past, present and future were one in a timeless reality. To participate in this was to experience eternal life, a foretaste of the life of the age to come.

SALVATION

Baptism remained the essential beginning of the Christian life. Through it the believer received forgiveness and salvation, yet this gift might be lost through subsequent sin – a problem the earliest church had not had to consider. This acquittal was, however, already bestowed through repentance, faith and baptism, provided the believer thereafter abstained from 'mortal' sin. In the first three centuries opinion differed as to whether sin after baptism could be forgiven, but after the church became the religion of the Roman empire, its power to mediate forgiveness, particularly through the sacrament of confession, was unquestioned.

If salvation had originally been escape from an historical act of divine wrath, it had early become linked with acquittal from divine judgement. At first this had been judgement on a world alienated from God. When, through the growth of the church, most people (within the Roman empire at least) were baptised, judgement had to be related to post-baptismal life. It was thus increasingly seen as pronounced upon the individual at, or just after, death. Salvation, then, began in baptism, continued through Eucharistic life, but was only complete after death. The nature and means of this salvation became a matter of discussion. How could justice and mercy be reconciled?

THEORIES OF ATONEMENT

St Paul had used the imagery of the law court to expound the salvation offered in Christ. Death was the universal penalty for sin from the time of Adam. Since Christ was sinless, his death was undeserved. Those who were 'in Christ' might therefore claim that he had undergone the death which they deserved and so their penalty was already paid. In the many centuries of Christian history St Paul's account of salvation has been variously interpreted. Many 'theories of atonement' have been put forward to explain how Christ's death brings forgiveness and salvation. On one hand are those that have been classified as of an objective type. These regard the death of Christ as making a real change in humanity's relationship to God and, mostly, take St Paul's juridical metaphors very literally. Some speak of the Father's demand for justice which can only be satisfied by a real payment. Christ's death makes this payment, which is then credited to the account of those incorporate in him through faith or baptism: it propitiated the just wrath of the Father. Christ, as a substitute, paid the price of sin on behalf of sinners. The difficulty of such a theory is that, though one person can pay another's debts, justice is hardly satisfied by punishing one person for another's offences. Despite this the objective, substitutionary type of theory is still immensely popular in evangelical churches. The redeeming power of the Cross is treated as a fact, in which the convert is invited to put faith. Much effort is typically expended in making this rationally coherent: yet the theory has this glaring logical flaw. It appeals to justice and yet is unjust. In terms of bi-logic every effort seems to be made to make it rational and consonant with asymmetric logic: yet, at its heart, is irresoluble paradox – which no doubt explains its considerable power of appeal to the emotions.

Subjective theories of atonement have been put forward to avoid the difficulties of the objective type. These generally stress the exemplary force of Christ's sacrifice. As an act of love it appeals to the believer and draws others to imitate it. Yet if the death of Christ does not bring some objective benefit to others, then it is by no means clear why it is worthy of imitation. To lose one's life in saving another's is admirable: but merely to drown oneself because others are drowning appears futile. The exemplary theory was first expounded as a full account of redemption by Peter Abelard in the twelfth century and was adopted wholeheartedly by many liberal Protestants in the nineteenth century, who welcomed its appearance of straightforward rationality: it avoided the primitive-sounding notions of sacrifice and propitiation. Nevertheless, the subjective, exemplary theory, like the first type, rests on paradox. Both types of theory are intended to be rational, yet are at heart equally irrational.

Gustav Aulen, in his well-known work, *Christus Victor*,[1] discussed both types of atonement theory and concluded both were inadequate. He argued strongly that the patristic doctrine followed neither pattern. Indeed it was not so much a theory as a description, couched in mythical terms, of a conflict between God and the devil. Humankind had been in the power of the devil through sin and the devil had therefore rightfully inflicted the penalty of death. By putting the sinless Christ to death it had exceeded its rights, and therefore forfeited them altogether. The death of Christ therefore paid a debt, not so much to the justice of the Father, as to the Devil, a payment which ransomed humankind from the devil's grip. Aulen argued that no rational explanation of the atonement was possible. The story simply had to be accepted in full mythical dress. He claimed that this was St Paul's understanding of it, for in St Paul we find the Cross described as a victory over the powers of evil and the imagery of the imperial Roman triumph appears to be used to celebrate it.[2] According to Aulen, this understanding of the Cross as primarily a victory over the Devil passed on into the patristic period and it was revived with immense emotional power by Luther. Luther's followers, however, soon succumbed to the spirit of the times and returned to the apparently more rational objective theory. Supposed fact displaced myth. The fifth modality was rejected in favour of the appearance of reason.

Eastern Christianity in the Orthodox churches has paid little attention to theories of atonement and has remained at ease with the mythical language. At the same time it has strongly emphasised the Incarnation as redemptive in itself: because God became human in Christ, humanity in principle is set on the way to becoming God. Atonement – which at root is simply 'at-one-ment' – is thus an instance of the second law of symmetric logic: because God has become human, humanity has become divine.

The first clear statement of an objective theory is generally attributed to St Anselm[3] in eleventh-century France. Possibly the Roman inheritance of precise, legal thinking was responsible for the Latin-speaking West's desire to tie down the mythical thinking which, to the Greek church, was less problematic. The effect of (asymmetric) reasoning upon myth in the West seems to have been destructive. The theories of both types purported to be reasonable, yet contained contradictions. The objective type claimed as fact what cannot possibly be known: cosmic transactions in pursuit of an illusory justice. The subjective type ended up with nothing more to proclaim than the power of good example. More sophisticated versions of both arguments have been propounded. They have generally alleviated the objectionable features of the crude form by stressing a moral, spiritual or mystical union between the believer and Christ. At their best, either kind makes sense only if the identification of the believer with Christ is stressed to the utmost. A well-known Eucharistic hymn by the Victorian William Bright exemplifies this:

> And having with us him that pleads above,
> We here present, we here spread forth to thee
> That only offering perfect in thine eyes,
> The one true, pure, immortal sacrifice.
> Look, Father, look on his anointed face,
> And only look on us as found in him ... .[4]

The original sacrifice of Christ, though unique, is yet spread forth and presented anew, and the Father is asked to see the Christian only as he or she is 'in Christ'. This, however, is to use the story of Christ as repeatable, re-enacted myth – for even though the sacrifice of Christ is described as unique, it is yet presented anew in the present. The rationality of the objective theory is actually illusory: mythical and symmetric thinking are dominant.

The story, as repeated by the church, became dominated by the modalities. Its place, therefore is in transitional space, and the criteria for its truth, if there are any, are not those of historical fact. It became a story to be re-enacted by believers so as to create and reinforce its place in the zone of interchange between unconscious and conscious thinking. As it became a myth, the central actors subtly change. The Passion of Christ, if the Gospels are substantially correct, was a transaction between the man Jesus, Pontius Pilate and the Roman authorities, the Jewish Sanhedrin and those who worked for them, and his disciples including the traitor Judas. It became a cosmic contest between God and the Devil, in which all the rest were merely agents of these universal powers. In the process of its transformation, as we have suggested already, Jesus took on the attributes of God, an everlasting and ubiquitous figure, who came to be seen as paradoxically both God and man.

As an aside, it is worth noting that Christianity has never much considered the debt owed, not by humanity to God, but by God to humanity. I have suggested that, hidden in the story of Cain, is the thought that the choice of Abel was unjust and that God acknowledged that implicitly in his protection of Cain. Even the One, acting in time, cannot act with a total even-handed symmetry: and it is a matter of common observation that 'life' is not just. If God, too, bears guilt, then just as God died on the Cross to expiate human guilt, so, too, we might see there a human dying to expiate divine guilt. This is a thought developed by Carl Jung.[5]

THE DOCTRINE OF THE TRINITY

To examine the divinity of Christ we need to take a step back, and begin with the divinity of the Father. This discussion will also advance our understanding of the Consciousness of God. According to Mircea Eliade, the original theophany, the first revelation of the divine, was the sky itself.[6] The sky-gods of the ancient world were personifications of this primary disclosure, and among them stands the God of Israel.

The God who presides over the Old Testament is enthroned upon the Cherubim and his footstool is the Ark of the Covenant in the Temple in Jerusalem. The God experienced in the naked perception of the infinite bowl of the sky is anthropomorphised as stories are told of his engagement in terrestrial affairs. Jung, it may be noted, describes the Father-God as a personification in the Unconscious of the Unconscious itself.[7] When this personification is disclosed in Consciousness, a revelation is given by the Unconscious which tells something of itself. I am disposed to follow this line of thinking and to observe that the modalities, which in ultimate form are applicable only to the Unconscious, are found penultimately in speaking of this archetype: whereas the One is timeless, placeless, and ineffable, the image of the Father is everlasting, omnipresent, symbolic, paradoxical and spoken of in myth.

As the story of Christ became a myth, Jesus, as already discussed began increasingly to be spoken of in the modalities. It remained a story of a man's life, death and resurrection, but, as well, it became a story of a divine something becoming incarnate. The Word, that was from the beginning, became flesh. A man filled with the Spirit of God, as in Mark 1, was also an Incarnation of the Word. The Son of God was the Eternal Son in human form. Christ, already in St Paul, is pre-existent and, in the Prologue to St John's Gospel, he is with God in the beginning and 'all things were made through him, and without him was not anything made that was made'.[8] In the same Gospel Jesus proclaims that 'the Father and I are one'.[9] As the Church left its Jewish roots behind and became embedded in Hellenistic culture the question of the unity of God became an issue. Was God the Father God alone, or was the Son God also? If so were there two Gods? If not, how could he be both two and one? The mythic drama of salvation appeared to involve at least two divine actors – the status of the Spirit was a matter of less passionate controversy – and one diabolic actor, yet the overwhelming weight of biblical witness pointed to a single God and the Hellenistic philosophical tradition too demanded that the ultimate One be one, not two or three or many.

Platonistic and Gnostic Christians evolved schemes in which emanation is a prominent concept. The ultimate One remained remote and uncontaminated by multiplicity, yet from it emanated another, and sometimes through many stages, ultimately an emanation from an emanation was allowed to enter the material universe. Some of the early theologians of the church followed this line to a degree and 'subordinationist' theories of God were propounded. As a consequence of the Arian heresy there arose the claim that the Son was of *like* substance with the Father from whom he was begotten. However, the post-Arians believed that the Son was born in time. The orthodox, who held the Son was of the *same* substance as the Father, coined a slogan which denied this, 'There was not a time when he was not'.[10] The Son, like the One itself, was to be accorded the modality of timelessness in ultimate form.

The Father was the One, but the Son was begotten by him and the Spirit came from the Father through the Son, and thus the unity of God was preserved, while the Son was yet a divine figure. The Father was God, the Son was God and the Holy Spirit was God; yet there were not three Gods, but one.[11]

This conclusion is profoundly paradoxical. Nevertheless, from its origins in the controversies of the third, fourth and fifth centuries, to its modern adherents attempts have been made to make it rationally defensible, if not comprehensible. Greek ontology was stretched to its limits, and beyond, in this enterprise. Simple solutions, such as God having three parts, were impossible, since the One is essentially without parts. Nor would it do to see the three as different modes of the One, for each of the three was real as such, not simply an appearance or phase of the One. The formula adopted has been interpreted as 'three distinct objective forms' in 'one identical object'.[12] In the Latin-speaking church this became three Persons in one Substance, where the word 'person' had something of the meaning of 'mask'. Yet it did not mean what the English words suggest, for 'three persons' suggests three distinct entities and that is wrong: and 'three masks' suggest one person with different appearances; and that, too, is wrong. Nor could Godhead be conceived as a kind of common property of three different actual realities, for Godhead was not allowed to be a property of anything except the one God.

Ontology failed to make rational what the doctrine of the Trinity asserted, that three could be absolutely and completely one, and yet be distinctly, also, three. Symmetric logic, however, has no difficulty with this problem whatever: indeed it is apt to impose such 'amalgamations', even when all the factual evidence denies it. To the Unconscious, a present manager, a past teacher and an original parent, all people holding authority, are more than likely to be amalgamated in an indistinguishable, single figure. Likewise three divine 'persons' are, at a deep level, one God.

The doctrine of the Trinity is indeed incomprehensible to the rational mind, yet well-attuned to unconscious thinking. Driven by unconscious forces, events recalled in story became myth, and these same forces drove the myth into the total paradoxes of doctrine.

An interesting account of this period is given by Karen Armstrong in her recent book *A History of God*.[13] She underlines a distinction made by some theologians of the patristic age between the *kerygma*, or preaching, of the church, which was in mythical form, and the *dogma*, or inner mystical teaching, in which the absolute mystery of God is discussed in terms of Trinitarian doctrine. In the preaching, the story of Christ could be told as though Father, Son and Spirit were separate, though of course co-operating, entities. Once the divinity of Son and Spirit was established, the preaching gives the appearance of tritheism, belief in three gods. Meanwhile, the mystical teaching, as always, demands the unity of the One. In bilogical terms therefore, the preaching is more asymmetric, the dogma more symmetric. The preaching distinguishes the different roles of Father, Son and Spirit: the dogma passes beyond such distinctions to an inner unity. Both are in transitional space, but the dogma is moving persistently towards affirming the mystical unity.

A consequence of this pressure is the paradoxical doctrine that in any action of God towards the world all three Persons are equally involved. The preaching tells of a Creator, a Saviour and a Sanctifier, each of whom came to be seen as God. Belief in 'a three' arose from the different roles of Father and Son in the story of Christ. Yet later thought concluded that the Creator also saves and sanctifies, the Saviour also creates and sanctifies, the Sanctifier also creates and saves. The distinctions between Father, Son and Spirit are real only within God himself and to God himself: the Father eternally 'begets' the Son, and the Spirit eternally 'proceeds' from the Father (and, in Latin theology, from the Son as well). In relationship to the world, therefore, the Trinity perfectly expresses the third law of symmetric logic described in Chapter 3, the law of rotation.[14] The mystical thrust of the theologians has thus imposed upon such asymmetries as remained in the myth this further very comprehensive symmetry.

As to the distinctions within the Trinity, of begetting and proceeding, these are real yet, to a degree, qualified by the mysterious doctrine of co-inherence. Each person wholly indwells each other, and each is wholly indwelt by each other. Thus between each pair within the Trinity the symmetric law of reflection is dominant, save only for 'begetting' and 'proceeding'.

Preaching – and piety – talk in tritheistic terms of a three, yet dogma overwhelmingly proclaims a one, in which there is left the merest shadow of differentiation. Strangely, the arguments used throughout the patristic period and again in scholasticism appear highly rational. Yet the conclusions are utterly irrational. The argument is apparently driven both by philosophical considerations and by the desire to be faithful to the text of Scripture. Yet, I propose that in reality deep unconscious forces are steering the discussion in accordance with the laws of symmetric logic. A document of some importance historically is the statement known as the Athanasian Creed, which I quote below. I suggest to the reader that an attempt to study it will result only in puzzlement, but if it is read aloud as a kind of incantation (or still better, sung to Gregorian chant) one may sense that something powerful is at work, though what, one cannot easily say.

And the Catholick Faith is this: That we worship one God in
Trinity, and Trinity in Unity:
Neither confounding the Persons: nor dividing the Substance.
For there is one Person of the Father, another of the Son: and
another of the Holy Ghost.
But the Godhead of the Father, of the Son, and of the Holy Ghost,
is all one: the Glory equal, the Majesty co-eternal.
Such as the Father is, such is the Son: and such is the Holy Ghost.
The Father uncreate, the Son uncreate: and the Holy Ghost
uncreate.
The Father incomprehensible, the Son incomprehensible: and the
Holy Ghost incomprehensible.
The Father eternal, the Son eternal: and the Holy Ghost eternal.
And yet there are not three eternals: but one eternal.
As also there are not three incomprehensibles, nor three uncre-
ated: but one uncreated and one incomprehensible.[15]

The modern Christian is likely to have more sympathy with the
prayers of the Celtic saints than with the Athanasian Creed. In these
the philosophical terminology is dropped – there are no substances,
presentations of being, persons or natures. What is left is just 'the
One and the Three'. The effect is perhaps to create some kind of
reconciliation of feeling between kerygma and dogma, the mind
moving between the myth and the mystery at will. The hymn
ascribed to St Patrick illustrates this:

> I bind unto my self today
> The strong name of the Trinity,
> By invocation of the same,
> the Three in One and One in Three.[16]

A modern prayer, by David Adam, conveys this Celtic characteristic
even better:

> I bow before the Father
> Who made me
> I bow before the Son
> Who saved me
> I bow before the Spirit
> Who guides me
> In love and adoration
> I give my lips
> I give my heart
> I give my mind
> I give my strength

I bow and adore thee
Sacred Three
The Ever One
The Trinity.[17]

The doctrine of the Trinity is a summary of the Christian faith, in which the determining myth of Christianity is pushed into its most symmetric form. The One is one and yet is three-fold. Symmetry is all but wholly dominant, the very circumscribed threeness remains to represent multiplicity. This threeness might be seen as a reminder that the One is not the Gnostic Monad utterly distinct from the Many, but is itself the bestower of the desire for the unity of the Many in the One. It therefore affirms what the mystics have discovered in their journeys and described as a sense of cosmic unity and love.

THE DOCTRINE OF THE INCARNATION

Symmetric logic makes unities out of things apparently different. Father, Son and Holy Spirit became one in the doctrine of the Trinity. The unity of the Eternal Father and the Eternal Son was thus resolved. A second problem was how the Eternal Son was present in the human Jesus. Again patristic thinking approached this with an ontology intended to be rational, yet actually reinforcing the irrational. Salvation, in the patristic period, was seen as achieved by God becoming human and thereby making the human divine. The difficulty can be crudely summarised as follows: only God could save, so the Saviour must be wholly God. Yet God could only save what he 'assumed' in Jesus, so Jesus must be wholly human.

Rational solutions, as with the Trinity, led to errors. Thus any division of Jesus into a divine part and a human part was rejected — for then the human part would not be saved. Thus, Jesus could not have a human mind and a divine soul for example: he had to be a complete human being. Yet also he was wholly God. The 'solution' was found in the notion that he was one 'Person' or one 'concrete presentation of being' in two natures, divine and human. Some things that he did, he did on account of his human nature: eating, sleeping, dying. Others he did on account of his divine nature: working miracles, saving the world, rising from the dead. Yet, by virtue of the doctrine known as *communicatio idiomatum*[18] what he did in either nature might be said of the other — so that God was born and died, humanity was omnipotent and omniscient. The doctrine, as ontology, defies reason. As the work of symmetric logic — an identification of Godhead and humanity in Christ — it is what would be expected of all symmetric logic, patterned irrationality.

CHRIST AND THE CHRISTIAN

A third unity is central to Christian faith, the unity of Christ and believer. Once again, some have written of an ontological change effected by baptism, through which the very nature of humanity is changed. To a world without an ontology this is a difficult matter to understand and the notion that baptism, even with faith, makes such a change seems magical. The identification of the believer with Christ may, instead, be seen as effected by symmetric logic – whereas the continuing distinctness (emphasised by the reality of sin) expressed by asymmetric logic accounts for the obvious difference between the historical Jesus who lived in Palestine and the actual reality of the individual's existence today.

THE BODY OF CHRIST IN THE EUCHARIST

The loss of ontology is nowhere clearer than in discussion of the nature of the consecrated bread and wine of the Eucharist. The mediaeval and reformation debates about this require a notion of substance foreign to the modern mind. The nineteenth-century Anglican Bishop, who believed that the invention of a sufficiently powerful microscope would enable one to see if the Eucharistic bread was really the Body of Christ, expressed this loss perfectly. A unity of substance to him, and to most people today, is a matter of physics or chemistry. To the Scholastics, material properties are simply the 'accidents' of an object, with which substance is in contrast. 'Accidents' are what sense perception may be aware of, shape, colour, size and chemical composition. Substance in the mediaeval sense meant an underlying reality not of a material nature at all. If the bread of the Eucharist was changed into the Body of Christ substantially, this did not affect its material properties. It meant something more like a change in what it was to the eye of God. We might see this as equivalent to a change in the unconscious significance of it. Asymmetric thinking today is likely to stay with material considerations – with the accidents. Symmetric thinking is not constrained by these. To those, therefore, for whom the consecrated bread and wine participate in the reality of Christ, they are symmetrically identified with his body and blood.

SYMMETRY AND THEOLOGY

Vast areas of past Christian controversy are illuminated by investigating the bi-logic of the arguments. Every attempt to make rational the deliverances of unconscious thought has failed to catch something of that thinking; one side or other of a paradox has been played down, for example. This then has led to an opponent emphasising the other side of the paradox. Theology is much concerned with the unity of what appears different: God and Jesus, Jesus and his followers, the Risen Christ and the Consecrated Elements of the Eucharist: these 'unities' have particularly led to bitter controversies. Bi-logic is concerned with sameness and difference, with unity and separateness, and is therefore peculiarly suited to unravelling the threads of theological discussion – and knitting them together again. Many of the historic controversies of Christianity may be resolved by accepting the necessity of expressing them through paradox and myth, by recognising the symmetric logic implicit in all talk of God.

There are hints in the doctrines of the Trinity and Incarnation that something more may be claimed of the relationship between symmetric logic and theology. If, in a fundamental sense, God and the Unconscious are one and the same, then in these two doctrines can be found, in disguised dress, the laws of rotation and reflection, the three in one, and the two in one. Perhaps this is what is celebrated in the Greek Orthodox liturgy when the celebrant approaches the altar bearing two candlesticks: one two-branched; the other three-branched. Perhaps he is simply celebrating the symmetry of God.

12   Mythical Speaking

Faith speaks of a God who acts in the present lives of believers, as well as in the great events of revelation. Does this help us to find the conscious aspect of God? In this chapter the notions of providence, petitionary prayer, grace and life after death are discussed in search of divine action in the present. Once again, the Consciousness of God proves to be elusive.

We take up the search for the asymmetric aspect of God in another area of the language of faith. The beginning time of creation and the end time of the kingdom took us only into transitional space. The revelation of God in Christ appeared at first more particular, but we find, in fact, that faith handles even this as essentially in the same space. What, at first sight, sounds particular and definite rapidly recedes into the mist of the Great Time. What, then, does faith say of God's action in the present, in the events of our own lives?

GENERAL PROVIDENCE

The doctrine of divine providence seems a promising area for investigation. There is a long tradition behind the view that God is active in every detail of life. 'Even the hairs of your head are all counted',[1] said Jesus. It might be thought that here at last we must come upon very specific, particular acts of God, described therefore in asymmetric logic. At once, however, a difficulty arises: if every event is providential, then no event is specifically providential, and providence becomes a general property of everything. It is to events what creation is to objects, a general statement of relatedness to God. Creation, I have argued, as a general property of everything, rests upon a metaphor; an analogy, between, perhaps, a potter moulding a pot and God moulding each individual creature. Similarly, a doctrine of a general providence expresses another concealed metaphor: it suggests that just as a person may bring about some specific event, so also God brings specific events about – but none more specifically than any other. The doctrine tells us nothing of how God brings events about, nor as to which is more particularly his doing than any other. The reductionist might argue that, therefore,

136

the doctrine tells us nothing at all. But the doctrine does offer a metaphor by which our understanding of everything may be influenced, even though it does not explain why one thing happens rather than another. Once again therefore we find a promising lead in our search for the asymmetric aspect of God actually leads back towards symmetry. Belief in general providence does not describe a specific activity of God, but is rather a metaphor expressing God's interest in his creation in a very general way.

SPECIAL PROVIDENCE AND PRAYER

Beside the notion of a general providence, many believe in more specific providential actions of God. Those who believe in the power of prayer, for example, often claim that specific events are directed by God in response to human petition. As Jesus said, 'Ask and you will be given ... .' [2] A simple believer may imagine him- or herself to be in direct conversation with a loving divine Father as such prayers are spoken. This imagining requires a Consciousness in God analogous to human consciousness, a Consciousness moreover that is at that moment directed to the one who prays. Even the simplest of believers may at times be troubled by the difficulty of imagining a God who is instantly attentive to the prayers of each and every one of the two billion Christians in the world simultaneously. It is of the nature of human consciousness that it is focussed on one thing at a time and a more than Argus-eyed being capable of focusing simultaneously on millions of situations is unimaginable. The attempt to imagine God in converse with the believer is somewhat self-defeating, since it so quickly leads to the unimaginable: yet many see this as central to faith, of the essence of that personal relationship which is often claimed to be saving. Any attempt to take this imagining literally seems to lead immediately to impossibilities.

Leaving the latter, possibly rather trivial, point aside, the issue is whether prayer brings about specific consequences springing from a specific divine intervention. If such were the case there would appear to be a conflict with the notion of divine foreknowledge. If God's intervention depends upon human prayer then it is hard to see how this can fail to contradict the notion of divine foreknowledge. Of course both the prayer and the intervention might be foreknown, but then they lose their specific quality and become, like all other events, ordered from the beginning. However, a bi-logical approach allows us to evade this difficulty. Foreknowledge is an attribute of the symmetry of God, specific involvement, if it happens, would be a property of his asymmetry.

Petitionary prayer in the Scriptures, as noted before, often begins with the word 'Remember'. More strikingly than any other feature of the language of faith, this suggests the concept of a consciousness in God, analogous to human consciousness. The analogy demands that attention is directed here and there, that things enter and leave the conscious mind of God.

There are many – of literalist tendency – for whom this notion of God is acceptable and for whom prayer is intended to bring about events which otherwise would not happen. That concept might, without prejudice, be described as a paranormal concept of prayer. It implies that prayer can bring about consequences in the external world by means beyond the current reach of scientific explanation. Such a phenomenon is close to telepathy and telekinesis and ultimately may be proved or disproved by appropriate tests. Whether it happens or not is beyond our present scope. If it does, it suggests, indeed, that God has an asymmetrical aspect expressed in such paranormal activity.

There are many others for whom such a notion of petitionary prayer is less acceptable. There are reductionists who see it as incredible and magical. Some see it as actually immoral, an aspiration of believers to have access to a privileged source of power to bring about their wishes. Very many, including some whose writings on prayer are highly esteemed, adopt an intermediate position which might be summarised as follows. To ask is good, and commanded by Christ. Yet the expectation is not that the request will be immediately granted. Rather, the asking is seen as a step towards the prayer of Christ, 'Not my will but thine be done.'[3] The request is made more to clarify desire than to change the course of events. This, in turn, is a step towards changing the desire of the one who prays, in order that his or her will may be transformed into the will of God. Seen in this light, petitionary prayer is not an attempt to change directly the events of the external world. It is a process of purification of the will, of purging selfishness by bringing the particular within the scope of universal love and justice.

COINCIDENCE

Those who believe in specific interventions of God often talk of coincidences as confirmations of that belief. 'I lost my job, I had a car accident, and I heard a religious talk on the radio calling for deeper service to God – all in the same day. Then I knew God was calling me', is a typical expression of such an experience. This may be explained by the second law of symmetric logic, by which the Unconscious reverses relationships: a sequence of causes and effects becomes simultaneous. A sequence is therefore *coincidentally* present to the Unconscious, just as would be a number of events which in reality were coincidental.[4] The Unconscious can therefore not distinguish between a causative sequence and a coincidence. Thus, the one may be confused with the other and, under unconscious influence, coincident events may be understood to be causally related. Coincidence often strikes even the non-religious person as somehow uncanny. One disposed to believe in divine causation will readily see in it the hand of God.

GRACE

Believers often claim that divine interventions occur in the outward events of their lives. It seems that this belief is expressed in terms more symmetrical than might at first seem to be the case. However, far more religiously important than such occurrences is the intervention of God in the heart and soul and mind. Such interventions are often described as grace. The grace of forgiveness, of a change of heart, of repentance, of a power to love, etc. These changes are patently of an inward and psychological nature, by any account, and require no alleged distortion of the web of physical causation. Such changes take place at unconscious levels as well as conscious, and indeed are only effective if they do take place at unconscious levels. For example, the inner story which tells someone that they are always in the wrong needs to be displaced by an inner story which tells of forgiveness. These changes are typically brought about by the influences of words, of stories, though human friendship and acceptance may be an essential concomitant. The primary mode of divine action is therefore, not through paranormal happenings, but through the influence of the Gospel story. As the first letter of St Paul puts it, 'Let the word of Christ dwell in you richly.'[5] God acts through the rich indwelling story.

The means by which God imparts gifts of grace may then be summarised as follows: the Unconscious has shaped stories which, working in the mode of myth, change the inner convictions of the believer about him- or herself. There is no need to conceive the imparting of grace as a kind of spiritual injection direct from God to the human soul. Grace is the effect of myth; the means by which it communicates are the modalities working at unconscious levels, deep speaking to deep.

MYTHICAL SPEECH

This account of divine action may seem to destroy that converse with God which believers have often seen as essential to Christian life.

Such converse seems to require a belief in a directly intervening God, concerned about the details of daily living. This difficulty may be overcome if we conceive of a manner of speaking and thinking which might be called mythical speech. For example, in a traditional form of the service of Compline a prayer may be found which begins:

> Visit, we beseech thee, O Lord, this dwelling, and drive far from it all the snares of the enemy; let thy holy angels dwell herein to preserve us in peace.

There may be some who have used this prayer literally believing in the snares of the Devil and in the guardianship of angels, but it communicates a sense of security to many others who do not hold such a belief. Mythical speaking loses its efficacy if one tries to analyse it factually. In using such a prayer one might be imagining horned devils and winged angels, but one does not need to know what exactly they are, or indeed whether they have some kind of independent, concrete existence.

Mythical speaking is, to an extent, a lost art in a world dominated by scientific ontology. The literalist takes myth literally and fills the world with alleged facts, which do not stand critical examination. The reductionist tries to eliminate these from religion in the hope that it will then pass the test of reason: but thereby the language of faith is so impoverished that it communicates no longer. The recovery of a sense of ease with mythical speaking is therefore crucial to the survival of faith.

Mythical speaking includes the reciting of myth, the telling of the Christian story. It may encompass much more than that. The language of liturgy is where mythical speaking is most at home. Anthony Bloom wrote:

> A church, once consecrated, once set apart, becomes the dwelling-place of God. He is present there in another way than in the rest of the world. In the world he is present as a stranger, as a pilgrim, as one who goes from door to door, who has nowhere to rest his head; he goes as the lord of the world who has been rejected by the world and expelled from his kingdom and who has returned to it to save his people. In church he is at home, it is his place. He is not only the creator and the lord by right but he is recognised as such. Outside it he acts when he can and how he can; inside a church he has all power and all might and it is for us to come to him.[6]

What Bloom wrote of God is equally true of myth and mythical speaking. Our inner stories are indeed lords of our lives, and if the

Christian myth reigns in the inner soul it is lord and creator of our values and feelings. Yet the stories that express it may not be at home in everyday life, where the imaginings that accompany them are apt to be misinterpreted as fact or rejected as fiction.

LIFE AFTER DEATH

For many, Christian faith is intimately associated with the fear of mortality and the hope of life beyond death.[7] Once again the tyranny imposed by the need for factual knowledge leads some to false claims of certainty, and others to the abandonment of faith as unbelievable. The truth is that no one knows whether there is life beyond the grave, as literally pictured by many. Mythical speaking about it abounds in Christian tradition. As an example, I quote Peter Abelard's hymn. It begins:

> O What their joy and their glory must be,
> Those endless sabbaths the blessed ones see!
> Crown for the valiant; to weary ones rest;
> God shall be all, and in all ever blest.[8]

Reward for those who have valiantly struggled, rest for the weary, and the hope of reunion with the dear departed are all part of this vision. The modalities, however, are strongly present. 'There dawns no sabbath, no sabbath is o'er', expresses timelessness – it is always Sunday, and indeed always noon on Sunday if we borrow from another hymn the lines, 'Endless noon-day, glorious noon-day, From the sun of suns is there.'[9] Paradox is apparent in the thought that while the blessed ones and the angels are still distinct beings, yet 'God shall be all'. The symbolism of the Monarch, with his court and throne abounds. Most striking of all is the clear expression of the identify of fantasy and reality, since 'Wish and fulfilment shall severed be ne'er, Nor the thing asked for come short of the prayer.'

Harps and angels, once the stock in trade of the preacher at funerals, perhaps do not appeal to the imagination in the way that once they did. The modern funeral oration is more likely to be effective if it contains mythical speaking of a less ornate kind. The notably cantankerous dead may be imagined complaining of conditions in the heavenly Jerusalem, or the inveterate 'workaholic' as looking out for odd jobs. I have often observed such references causing humour and creating warmth at funeral services, the warmth including a sense of safety in the face of death. They express belief in continued life, but with a contrafactual absurdity that partakes of the modality of paradox. More important, they include the deceased as he or she was known in life within the myth of the heavenly Jerusalem. They are thus a way of speaking mythically about a particular person. Because myth belongs in transitional space, close to the seat of the emotions, they have the power of that space to express and release feeling. Because transitional space is where values are most deeply expressed, speaking mythically of the departed is a way of being in touch with their importance to us: its validity does not depend upon alleged factual knowledge of an 'after-life'.

THE CONSCIOUSNESS OF GOD

A purely rational assessment of mythical speaking might well consign it to the realm of make-believe. Those who choose to do that are, however closing a highway to the Unconscious. Since even rationality rests upon values formed by feeling and originating in the Unconscious, this choice ultimately divorces consciousness from its unconscious source and spring.

Those who believe in the reality of paranormal phenomena accompanying faith may claim that such phenomena are evidence for a personal God, a supreme Being, an existing Someone who fulfils in concrete form the archetype of the divine Father. The question of the Consciousness of God is then answered. God exists in the full traditional theistic sense of a Mind behind the universe, a mind which I have described as both unconscious and conscious.

To those who are uncertain or sceptical about paranormal phenomena, another view is possible, which transcends the certainties of both traditional theism and atheism. In this view, the Consciousness of God is not to be identified with the consciousness of the divine entity for whose existence metaphysical theists have generally argued. The Unconscious of God may be defined as that to which the mystics journey, but his Consciousness is altogether more elusive. We might speculate that when God is all in all, then all humanity, and all creation, will share a single consciousness. In the meantime we could speak of the Consciousness of God as being in the process of formation as hints of it appear in the consciousness of human beings. The Christian will want to claim that it pre-eminently appeared in the consciousness of the human Jesus. The 'group mind'[10] brought into being by the presence of the Holy Spirit might also be a manifestation of the Consciousness of God. It might be seen, too, wherever 'the kingdom God is very close': in situations where symmetry is expressed in the asymmetric particularities of human affairs, through justice and forgiveness. In other words, whenever people form among themselves 'the mind of Christ', as St Paul enjoined, there is the Consciousness of God.

Whether the Consciousness of God will ever be fully manifest universally within history is another question. It is the same as asking whether the kingdom of God will come in its fullness upon earth. There are those who still believe in a sudden divine intervention of the kind that the earliest Christians expected. Others look to a gradual evolution of the world through benign historical progress that will lead finally to a transformation of it. Some vision of this latter sort seems implicit in the process theology deriving from Whitehead's philosophy.[11] It is also congruent with Teilhard de Chardin's vision[12] of a new stage of evolution, a step comparable to the evolution of life and to the emergence of human consciousness, in which a unity of consciousness comes into being – Cosmogenesis and the Omega Point. Such would be a 'group mind' of universal dimensions. Some may find this convincing, but others will take note of the ebb and flow of human affairs and conclude that the kingdom will always be an ideal vision which at different times is more or less realised in historical reality. Such will be content with the thought that myth will always be myth and never become fact.

In the meantime, before a universal human Consciousness comes into being, if ever it does, mythical speaking about the particularities of human affairs is in an ambiguous situation. It relates the very specific, about which asymmetric logic is appropriate, to the deep generalities of myth. That is its purpose. If it is misinterpreted as fact, all the falsities and, often, cruelties of pious, literal Christianity are likely to be released.

Mythical speaking about the particular therefore needs to express its ambiguity, its provisional nature, or it will be misunderstood. Humour, irony or implicit self-mockery are ways in which this may be done, and convey a hint of the modality of paradox – what is said is, at least implicitly, unsaid. This is not to deprive it of its proper seriousness. The answer of Shadrach, Meshach and Abed-nego to the king who threatened them with the burning fiery furnace is an excellent example:

If it be so, our God whom we serve is able to deliver us from the burning fiery furnace; and he will deliver us out of your hand, O king. But if not, be it known to you, O king, that we will not serve your gods or worship the golden image which you have set up.[13]

Mythical speaking connects the things of present life with the realm of myth. It is the language of a stranger in the hard world of fact; but used ironically, humorously, tentatively, tenderly, it graces reality with the poetry of myth.

There is one last way of speaking of God which needs briefly to be considered. When justice and forgiveness are under debate then direct, asymmetric speech is possible. Over these matters it is sometimes possible to declare without ambiguity what is the will of God. In these asymmetric particulars are addressed, in order to bring them into that balance which expresses the symmetry of total justice. It is sometimes possible to declare that certain things must be done to achieve this, to bring about a situation that can be described in bi-modal assertions, and which, therefore, brings nearer the mythical kingdom of God.

The conclusions of this chapter and the last may now be tabulated according to the degree of symmetry and asymmetry implicit in the language of faith.

Table 12.1 Symmetry and Asymmetry Implicit in the Language of Faith

Ultimate form:

The Unconscious of God is spoken of in the ultimate forms of the modalities. The formal Dogmas of the Trinity and Incarnation contain the first hints of asymmetry, but are still overwhelmingly expressed in ultimate forms

Penultimate form:

The myths of creation, salvation and the end are spoken of typically in penultimate forms.

Ante-penultimate form:

Mythical speaking, at first sight more asymmetrical, is expressed through the modalities, often in weak or hidden forms.

More asymmetrical speech:

The pursuit of justice and the practice of forgiveness are expressed in asymmetric logic. Through these the many are brought into harmony with one another and thereby express the symmetry of the One. The resulting state may be described in bi-modal assertions.

13   Orthodoxy and the Orthobola

From the first centuries of Christian history to the present day, theologians have tried to describe the nature of God in terms derived from philosophy. In the present time, when overarching philosophies express at best the beliefs only of small minorities, such an approach seems unlikely to be understood very widely. Rather than directly assaulting the problems of ontology and metaphysics we have instead examined how believers have actually used the concepts implicit in the creeds, scriptures and worship of the churches. In particular we have been concerned with the question of how much of this great wealth of language is to be taken literally, how much is purely fictional, and whether there is some middle way that transcends a judgement overweighted in either direction.

We have been concerned, above all, to argue that the historic faith of Christianity can still connect with the insights and experience of those not already committed to it. On one side there is a vision of faith of a conservative kind, which takes the assertions of faith very literally. It may win converts, but to those not persuaded by it, it seems to offer membership of a comfortable ghetto at the cost of intellectual integrity. It professes to know far too precisely what is essentially mysterious and unknowable. It is a view of faith we might call over-determined. This view of faith I have described as wrecked on the rock of Scylla.

On another side there is a reductionist tendency which ends by having little to say that those outside the church would not take for granted in any case. The language of faith becomes a kind of poetic fiction for those who like it. As a colleague once said to me, 'The reductionists may be right, but who would bother to get up early on a Sunday morning to celebrate what they proclaim?' To those outside it seems to deny exactly what they thought the church believed, and thereby confirms a view that the faith is no more than fairy stories.

The church, therefore, seems to be cut asunder by the sword of reason, a reason which demands that the assertions of faith be either literal fact or mere fiction. I have argued instead that the central beliefs of Christians are inherently neither fact nor fiction. If God is to be spoken of at all, if any intimations of the eternal and infinite that humankind receives are to be expressed, then necessarily their expression is paradoxical, symbolic and mythical. I reiterate that 'myth' as used here means something different from fiction.

The mythical, in this sense, is neither true nor false. Myths belong close to the horizon within which our conscious lives are lived and they express perceptions of the infinite and eternal. Our deepest emotions come from beyond that horizon and these shape our ultimate values, values which determine, among other things, what truth and falsity are for us. Myth is therefore at a level logically prior to the distinction between truth and falsity.

Myths are within us, both communally and individually, lodged beneath the seat of reason. They participate, to a degree, in the unchanging eternity of the Unconscious. Yet the individual's awareness of his or her internal myths may change. There may be a greater or lesser awareness of them in consciousness. Part of the journey of faith is to make them more explicit. This may occur dramatically and suddenly in a 'conversion experience' or gradually through a long slow process in which someone devotes long meditative attention to their inner myths. They may be found to be dysfunctional in their effects on daily living, and someone may want to escape from them. This may be attempted by adopting the myths of another culture, by a change of faith. Or the outward expression of them in religious ritual may be abandoned. Or in rare cases someone may go into psychoanalysis to be delivered from the influence of a myth experienced as malign. Or someone under the influence of a cult may undergo what outsiders describe as brainwashing. All these journeys of faith involve change in the relationship of the conscious mind to inner myth. They are seldom advanced primarily by purely rational argument nor by empirical evidence, though these often play some part in the discussion, and the discussion may be couched in terms of them. For the most part that will be a rationalisation of a process more driven by emotional and personal factors rooted in the Unconscious.

I presuppose that within everyone there are fundamental dispositions which determine our values, emotions, relationships and indeed every important matter in our lives. Of these we may or may not be conscious and of them no one is fully conscious.

These fundamental dispositions may be expressed in the form of embryonic story: 'I am always a loser', 'People are always against me', or, probably less commonly, the opposites of these. The territory in which these are grounded is the battle-ground upon which the Gospel story is at war with them.[1] It seeks to supplant such dispositions with its own message: 'God loves me', 'God is merciful and forgives',

'Sacrificial love as revealed in Jesus is ultimately victorious.' Such summary statements are powerless clichés in themselves, but clothed in their full mythic army, expressed through the modalities of transitional space, they may transform the springs of human feeling and action.

Yet myth, and mythical speaking, is full of dangers. The speculation proposed in Chapter 3 regarding the Orthobola and the diabolas is one way of understanding this. An over-determined concept of God which purports to speak of the ultimate depths in precise and factual terms lies on a diabola – and shares the same territory of the graph of Figure 3.1 (p. 39) as paranoid obsession. It is stuck upon Scylla. Of course, that does not imply that those who embrace that concept are mentally ill. It is, nevertheless, noteworthy that idolatry is regarded in Scripture as the worship of demons, and mental illness is seen as possession by demons.

On the other side of the Orthobola, at the other end of diabolas, lie concepts of God which are under-determined. That is to say that the fluidity of symmetric logic is applied, not to the ultimate Unconscious, which is its appropriate place, but to more conscious matters. For example, pleasing, conscious feelings may be identified with the Holy Spirit and an absolute and ultimate value placed upon them. This is the danger of the excessively charismatic expressions of faith which have appeal to many at this time. There is often a swift transition from a rigid fundamentalism to an extremely emotional faith, from Scylla to Charybdis, from one end of a diabola to the other.

The conviction from which this book proceeds is that orthodox Christianity, potentially at least, lies on the Orthobola. This is a matter as much of how beliefs are held, as of what those beliefs are. In such a faith, the ultimate things of God are known to be unknowable, glimpsed only in transcendental experience, expressed, as best they may be, by the mystical writers. Less ultimately, orthodoxy is expressed in the myths of creation, redemption and final consummation. These expressions are not to be held dogmatically as the only possible truth: they are confessed as what the company of believers has inherited and experiences as speaking truthfully. 'Mythical' truth is not decided by fact, but by experience: we talk of a bell 'ringing true', and of a 'good man and true' and it is in a similar sense that myths may be said to be true.

In mythical speaking, orthodox belief connects personal experience of daily living with the myth, through the language of formal worship and private prayer, through imaginative reflection upon Scripture and upon daily experience. Mythical speaking often suggests to the mind certain pictures – of a conscious, listening, divine Father, of the Son seated beside him, of angels and devils, of

providential or miraculous interventions, of life after death. The
human imagination may delight in such pictures and the forming of
them is entirely legitimate. If, however, believers suppose that there
is an underlying 'factual reality' that approximately corresponds to
those pictures, then they are giving a false concreteness to what is
essentially mysterious and unknowable. Mythical speaking suggests,
very often, the picture of a conscious, divine being – the
Consciousness of God. Many believers find this picture valuable:
there are others, perhaps mostly outside the church, who do not. The
assumption that the language of faith can only be used honestly by
those who take this picture somewhat literally needs to be rejected.
Likewise, mythical speaking often suggests pictures of life after death
in heaven of the kind that artists have painted through the ages. How
literally one understands these pictures is a matter of personal
decision: faith does not demand belief in the survival of death as
though it were a matter of factual truth. Mythical speaking, in short,
is not to be taken at face value, any more than is myth.

The language of faith is, however, to be taken at face value in the
practice of forgiveness and in the pursuit of justice. Here its assertions engage in a literal way with matters of fact. These, as much as
myths and doctrines, may be expressions of orthodox faith. Through
these faith becomes practical in its pursuit of the unity of humankind
in the kingdom of God. Indeed, it might be argued that the whole
edifice of mystical journey, doctrine, myth and mythical speech is
meaningless unless it does issue in such assertions. Many are therefore tempted by the possibility of dispensing with this edifice: Freud
is one of many, through the ages, who have warned us that human
motivation is a deep and complex matter. To ignore the depths is to
risk falling victim to the malignant forces which may proceed from
them. The struggle for the kingdom needs to be pursued on every
level of the mind.

I have used the Orthobola as a guide in the attempt to distinguish
orthodox faith from the dangers that beset it. To summarise, this
approach suggests that the most deep and mysterious matters are to
be spoken of with the least pretence of clear and factual knowledge –
the territory of mysticism. At a more conscious level we find myths.
They are confessed as the beliefs of a community, not asserted as
public truths. Only in the practical pursuit of justice are clear and
definite pronouncements to be declared as the mind of God – and
only then with care.

No church or Christian community has any right to claim such
'orthobolic' orthodoxy as uniquely its own. People of any faith may
well practise an 'orthobolic faith'. I write, however, from within the
Christian tradition and make no claim to speak for any other.

Within Christianity I have written of a popular vision of faith which is over-determined, which claims to know with certainty what cannot be known at all. A vision in which, while those who hold it claim to be in the service of God, yet really God is at their beck and call – the God who, in the well-known anecdote, will find the prayer group parking spaces in a busy street, but who will do nothing to restrain human violence or withhold natural disaster.

On the other hand, there is a liberal or reductionist tendency which hopes to deliver faith from its mythical fetters. As the great Austin Farrer said of it long ago, it may free faith of its fetters, but it does so by amputating the limbs as well.[2] Myth 'demythologised' is myth deprived of imagination.

As a new millennium dawns, parts of the world are torn about by adherents of competing myths, who see in them only the choice by 'God' of their own tribe. One who believes in no particular myth may believe the world would be better rid of them. Yet, on the other hand, particularly the Western world struggles to find eternal meaning in anything. It is often described as 'post-modernist' and we are told that the great stories are all dead. Meaning is to be found only in lesser goods and only for a passing hour. Humankind picks and chooses its values at the whim of the moment. To live in such a way is to live in the whirlpool of Charybdis, where the centre has been lost, and anything may claim to be the centre for a time. As the poet Yeats observed: 'Things fall apart; the centre cannot hold', and the consequence is that 'The best lack all conviction [Charybdis] while the worst / Are full of passionate intensity [Scylla].'[3]

The search for the Centre, the Unconscious, God, the One, or whatever else it may be called, is the search for ultimate meaning, beauty, justice, forgiveness, peace. The desire that impels it is surely universal, however it may be misinterpreted, or, for a time, forgotten. The ancient wisdom of the Christian faith has been renewed in every generation by new insight into that desire. Without such insights it falls victim to nostalgia or distortion. The work of Freud has been largely neglected by the Church, whose God he apparently misunderstood. Yet the understanding of the human soul that comes from him might be a great enrichment to the Christian faith. God is called the soul of our souls, the spirit within our spirits, and Freud was one of the great explorers of the soul. I would like Christians to awake to the challenge of the Freudian Unconscious, so that it may be said, in the famous words of John Donne:

They shall awake as Jacob did, and say as Jacob said, 'Surely the Lord is in this place', and 'This is no other but the house of God, and the gate of heaven'.

And into that gate they shall enter, and in that house they shall dwell, where there shall be no darkness nor dazzling, but one equal light; no noise nor silence, but one equal music; no fears nor hopes, but one equal possession; no foes nor friends, but one equal communion and identity; no ends nor beginnings, but one equal eternity.[4]

My argument has rested heavily on the mystics. A post-modernist outlook might see in them the adherents of the esoteric hobby of a tiny minority. I believe, on the contrary, that their insight is insight of universal value, without which humanity will lose its centre. It is a centre which is disclosed to most of us in 'transcendental moments'. These, too, may be dismissed, disregarded as inconsequential aberrations of the mind: or they may be treasured as glimpses of the centre. A people who have lost touch with their myths will be exposed to loss of the centre, for they will have no language to connect it with the rest of life. That is the role of myth and, derived from myth, of mythic speaking.

I have written this book in the conviction that the language of the Christian faith – the only faith I know from the inside – does not require belief counter to known fact and to reason working in its proper sphere. Nor does it require to be shorn of its imagery and its paradoxes to accommodate these. It is not contrary to fact and reason, but deals also with matters beyond them. I have hoped to show that there is a coherence between the different levels of that language: a coherence between the pursuit of justice, the words of prayer and liturgy, the great story of the myth of Christ, the insights of speculative doctrine, and the paradoxes of the mystic. At each level the same goal is implicit: to express, in the immeasurably complex variety of the particulars of life, the symmetry of God.

Notes and References

CHAPTER 1

1. Boulton, David, *A Reasonable Faith*, a booklet published by the Sea of Faith Network, 1996.
2. Bertram, Jerome, 'The Liberal and the Dogmatical', in *Updating God*, ed .W. Schwarz, Marshall, Morgan and Scott, Basingstoke, 1988.
3. Robinson, J.A.T., *Honest to God*, SCM Press, London, 1963.
4. Anon., *The Cloud of Unknowing*. I have used the Burns and Oates edition, edited by Abbott Justin McCann, London,1924.
5. Traherne, Thomas, *Poems, Centuries and Three Thanksgivings*, ed. Anne Ridler, Oxford University Press, London, 1966. I quote from p. 264, the 'Third Meditation of the Third Century'.
6. Ibid.
7. Felipe Fernandez-Armesto in *The Future of Religion*, Phoenix, London, 1997, uses as a test for valid religion, that which nourishes 'a sense of transcendence which genuinely reaches for the infinite and eternal', p. 2.
8. Eliot, T.S., 'Burnt Norton', *The Four Quartets*, Faber and Faber, London, 1944, 1.62.
9. St Thomas Aquinas, *Summa Theologiae*. I use T. McDermott's Concise Translation, which, for the non-specialist, makes Aquinas more accessible by omitting the complex structure imposed on the original by the conventions of mediaeval debate. This quotation is from p. 23.
10. Ibid.
11. Ibid., p.24.
12. Psalm 103.
13. Daniel 7:22.
14. St Mark 11:4.
15. St Luke 23:53.
16. Revelation 2:8.
17. Revelation 1:8.
18. St Augustine, *Confessions*, Book X, chap. 27.
19. Freud, Sigmund, 'The Unconscious', in James Strachey, ed. *The Standard Edition of the Complete Psychological Works of*

Sigmund Freud, 24 vols, London, Hogarth, 1953–73, vol. xiv, p. 187. I have taken the liberty of replacing the abbreviations 'system Ucs' and 'system Cs' by 'Unconscious system' and 'conscious system', respectively.

20. Freud, Sigmund, 'Moses and Monotheism'. Standard Edition, Vol. 4, p. 314, Hogarth, London. Freud's writings may be found conveniently in the Penguin Freud Library. This is in *The Origins of Religion*, translated by James Strachey, Penguin, London.
21. Jones, Ernest, *Sigmund Freud, Life and Work, Volume 3*, p. 386.
22. Freud, Sigmund, 'Beyond the Pleasure Principle, *On Metapsychology*, p. 299.
23. Freud, Sigmund, 'The Future of an Illusion', in *Civilisation, Society and Religion*, Penguin, London, 1991.

CHAPTER 2

1. Freud, Sigmund, 'A Difficulty in the Path of Psycho-Analysis', in James Strachey, ed. *The Standard Edition of the Complete Psychological Works of Sigmund Freud*, 24 vols, London, Hogarth, 1953–73, vol. XVII.
2. Robinson, J.A.T., *Honest to God*, SCM Press, London, 1963.
3. Ramsey, Michael, wrote a pamphlet in criticism, *Image Old and New*, which it is alleged he later regretted producing.
4. Freud, Sigmund, *The Future of an Illusion*. Standard Edition, Vol.14, p. 187, Hogarth, London.
5. Suttie, Ian D., *The Origins of Love and Hate*, Kegan Paul, London, 1935.
6. White, Victor, *God and the Unconscious*, Harvill Press, London, 1952.

CHAPTER 3

1. A simple account of these discoveries will be found in Stephen Hawking's *A Brief History of Time*, Bantam Press, London, 1988.
2. I have relied upon Henri Ellenberger's *The Discovery of the Unconscious*, Basic Books, New York, 1970, for an account of Pierre Janet's thinking and its influence upon Freud.
3. Matte Blanco, Ignacio, *The Unconscious as Infinite Sets*, Duckworth, London, 1975.
4. I have drawn the following biographical information from Eric Rayner's *Unconscious Logic*, Routledge, London, 1995. I have also borrowed extensively from this book to expound Matte Blanco's theories.

5. Matte Blanco, Ignacio, *Thinking, Feeling and Being*, Routledge, London, 1988.

6. Arithmetic computation fulfils this description, and mathematics is often presented in this way. The discovery of it is a very different matter, and Ramanujan, one of the greatest mathematical geniuses of the twentieth century, received many insights in dreams, products of unconscious process and transmission. See Robert Kanigel's *The Man Who Knew Infinity*, Charles Scribner's Sons, New York, 1991: 'after seeing in dreams the drops of blood that, according to tradition, heralded the presence of the god Narasimha, scrolls containing the most complicated mathematics used to unfold before his eyes' (p. 281).

7. See Rayner, note 4 above.

8. Matte Blanco, *The Unconscious as Infinite Sets*, p. 42.

9. Ibid., p. 38.

10. I quote Eric Rayner here, from a privately circulated paper.

11. In logic, 'not-p' normally means the simple negation of 'p'. Thus if p stands for *I like*, not-p means *I do not like*, which is not the same as *I dislike*. I do not follow this convention and consistently use 'not-' to denote what I have called 'opposition', not mere negation.

12. Karpman, Stephen, 'Fairy Tales and Script Drama Analysis', *Transactional Analysis Bulletin* 7, April 1968. I do not wish to support his application of this insight, however.

13. Shakespeare, William, *A Midsummer Night's Dream*, Act V, scene 1, line 22.

14. Bomford, Rodney, 'Mapping Mental Processes', *Journal of Melanie Klein and Object Relations* 16(1), March 1998, pp. 35–46.

15. Shakespeare, William, *A Midsummer Night's Dream*, Act V, scene 1, line 22. The passage is quoted above, p. 38.

16. Carvalho, Richard, 'Consciousness, Symmetry, and Affective Intensity in Bi-Logic', *Journal of Melanie Klein and Object Relations* 16(1), March 1998, pp. 47–60.

17. 'Transitional space' is a term with a number of uses. I do not intend any reference to, for example, Winnicott's use of the term, but wish it to be understood as defined here.

CHAPTER 4

1. Matte Blanco, Ignacio, *The Unconscious as Infinite Sets*, Duckworth, London, 1975, p. 41. In the pages following, Matte Blanco discusses all five characteristics in the light of symmetric logic.

2. Readers who are familiar with psychoanalytic literature will probably know Ella Freeman Sharpe's book, *Dream Analysis*, Hogarth Press, London, 1959. Her discussion of various figures of speech throws much further light on their importance in unconscious process.

3. From the *Sanctus*, a set section of the Eucharist in the Roman Catholic, Anglican and Orthodox churches, but originally to be found in Isaiah 6:3.

4. Psalm 69:5, as found in the Church of England's *Book of Common Prayer*, 1662.

5. Psalm 69:12.

6. St Matthew 20:16.

7. Eliot, T.S., 'Burnt Norton', lines 139-49 from *The Four Quartets*, Faber and Faber, London, 1944.

8. Fowler, H.W., *A Dictionary of Modern English Usage*, Oxford University Press, London, 1926, p. 601. The quotation is from Luke 16:3.

9. Fowler's article on 'Technical Terms' in his *Modern English Usage* p. 597ff, contains a number designated as rhetorical. For the most part these are tropes or figures of speech.

10. Ibid., p. 602. The quotation is from I Corinthians 2:9.

11. *The Alternative Service Book*, William Clowes, Colchester, 1980, p. 131.

12. Hanna Segal's paper 'Notes on Symbol Formation' is of great interest. She distinguishes sharply between symbolism and symbolic equations. In the former there is known to be difference between the symbol and the thing it represents: in the latter – as with what I have called identity – there is no awareness of the difference at all. The symbol is then felt to be the original object. *In Collected Works of Hanna Segal*, Aronson, New York, pp. 49–69.

13. Soskice, Janet, *Metaphor and Religious Language*, Oxford University Press, Oxford, 1985, p. 15.

14. Ibid., p. 57. She is quoting from *Somewhere I have Never Travelled*.

15. I owe this anecdote to Paddy O'Neil, the distinguished former Co-ordinator of the youth project, CARE-free.

16. Fowler, *Modern English Usage*, p. 612.

17. Ibid. p. 613.

18. I have not found the original source; it was quoted by Jonathan Harvey in 'An Approach to Church Music', *Musical Times*, January1980.

19. Job 1:21.

20. Shakespeare, William, *Macbeth*, Act II, scene 1.

CHAPTER 5

1. Genesis 28:12.
2. Van Ruysbroeck, The Blessed Jan, *The Seven Steps of the Ladder of Spiritual Love*, trans. F. Sherwood Taylor, Dacre Press, Westminster, 1944.
3. Johnston, William, *The Inner Eye of Love*, Collins, 1978, reprinted Fount Paperbacks, London, 1981, from which quotations are made here.
4. Ibid., p. 32.
5. Ibid., p. 38.
6. Ibid., p. 32.
7. Ibid., p. 127.
8. Ibid., p. 127.
9. Ibid., p. 31.
10. *The Cloud of Unknowing* and *The Epistle of Privy Counsel* are anonymous works of the same fourteenth-century author published in one volume by Burns and Oates, London, 1964 (Golden Library edition), ed. by Abbot Justin McCann.
11. *The Cloud*, p,.5.
12. *Privy Counsel*, p. 126.
13. Ibid., p. 121.
14. *The Cloud*, p. 43.
15. Meyendorff, John, *Byzantine Theology*, Fordham University Press, New York, 1974, and Mowbray, Oxford, 1975 (from which quotations are made), p. 27.
16. Ibid., p. 14. Meyendorff is quoting Gregory of Nyssa, 'Commentary on Ecclesiastes 3:7', trans. by H. Musurillo, in *From Glory to Glory: Texts from Gregory of Nyssa's Mystical Writings*, Scribner, New York, 1961.
17. Meyendorff, *Byzantine Theology*, p. 27.
18. Kapleau, Roshi Philip, in *The Three Pillars of Zen*, Anchor Books, explains the use of koans at some length. Well-known examples include, 'What is the sound of one hand clapping?', and 'The East Mountain strides over the water'.
19. *Privy Counsel*, p. 126.
20. *The Cloud*, p. 8.
21. Ibid., p. 7ff.

CHAPTER 6

1. Tillich, Paul, *Systematic Theology, Vol. 1*, James Nisbet, Welwyn, 1953, p. 11.
2. St Thomas Aquinas, *Summa Theologiae*, Concise Translation (T. McDermott), Faber and Faber, London, 1944, p. 22. E.L.

Mascall, discusses this in *He Who Is*, Longman, Green, London, 1943, p. 13, in a manner intelligible to the reader not used to Scholastic terminology.
3. St Thomas Aquinas, *Summa Theologiae*, pp. 12–14.
4. Macquarrie, John, *Principles of Christian Theology*, revised edition, S.C.M. Press, London, 1977, p. 49.
5. Mother Julian of Norwich, 'Sixteen Revelations of Divine Love', in *Julian of Norwich*, CIO Publishing, London, 1984, chapter 4.
6. See Chapter 1, p. 9, where this is quoted in context.
7. Blake, William, 'Auguries of Innocence,' in, e.g., *Complete Writings*, ed. G. Keynes, Oxford University Press, 1969, p. 431.
8. St Thomas Aquinas, *Summa Theologiae*, Editor's introduction, p. xxxi.
9. See Chapter 1, p. 10.
10. Probably the easiest place to find the Athanasian Creed is in the *Book of Common Prayer* (1662) of the Church of England. Much of it is quoted in Chapter 11 (p. 132).
11. St Thomas Aquinas, *Summa Theologiae*, p. 16.
12. *New English Hymnal*, Canterbury Press, Norwich, 1986, no. 521.
13. We speak of parts of us hurting, as in 'my finger is hurting', which comes near to saying, 'my finger is in pain'. But it is not the same: we might also say 'my finger is hurting me', and that sounds like a parallel to 'a splinter is hurting me', but of course it is rather different. The logic of 'hurting' and 'pain' is clearly not straightforward!

CHAPTER 7

1. Wittgenstein, Ludwig, *Philosophical Investigations*, trans. G.E.M. Anscombe, Blackwell, Oxford, 1958.
2. See Chapter 6, p. 68.
3. Lewis and Short, *Latin Dictionary*, *existere*.
4. Genesis 1:1–4.
5. Hawking, Stephen, *A Brief History of Time*, Bantam Press, London, 1988, p. 46.
6. Matte Blanco, Ignacio, *The Unconscious as Infinite Sets*; see Chapters 5 and 6.
7. Jung, Carl G., 'The Archetypes and the Collective Unconscious', *Collected Works*, Routledge and Kegan Paul, London, 1959, Vol.9, Part I, p.43.
8. Bettelheim, Bruno, *The Uses of Enchantment*, Thames and Hudson, London, 1976, p. 8.
9. Ibid., p .36.

10. Ibid., p.8.
11. I owe this illustration to my former colleague, Charles Pickstone.
12. Eliade, Mircea, *Patterns in Comparative Religion*, Sheed and Ward, London, 1958. For example, he writes:

> Thus, in New Guinea, when a master mariner went to sea he personified the mythical hero Aori: 'He wears the costume which Aori is supposed to have worn, with a blackened face and the same kind of *love* in his hair which Aori plucked from Iviri's head. He dances on the platform and extends his arms like Aori's wings' ... A man told me that when he went fish shooting he pretended to be Kivavia himself. He did not implore Kivavia's favour and help: he identified himself with the mythical hero. In other words, the fisherman lived in the mythical time of Kivavia just as the sailor identifying himself with Aori lived in the transhistoric time of that hero. (p. 394)

CHAPTER 8

1. See, for example, Mircea Eliade, The *Myth of the Eternal Return*, Penguin, London, 1989 (first published Bollingen Foundation, 1954), p. 16: 'the creation of man ... took place at a central point, at the centre of the world'.
2. Genesis 3:8.
3. Genesis 3:22.
4. Genesis 4:23ff.
5. Genesis 6:5.
6. Genesis 9:21–27.
7. Genesis 12:3.
8. Leviticus 26:12; also, Jeremiah 11:4.
9. Traherne, Thomas, *Poems, Centuries and Three Thanksgivings*, ed. Anne Ridler, Oxford University Press, London, 1966, 'First Century', para. 29.

CHAPTER 9

1. II Kings 19:35: 'the angel of the Lord went forth, and slew a hundred and eighty five thousand in the camp of the Assyrians'.
2. St Luke 2:32.
3. Isaiah 50:4–9 is perhaps the best example.
4. I Corinthians 15:20.
5. St Matthew 27:52: 'the tombs also were opened, and many bodies of the saints who had fallen asleep were raised'.

6. I Corinthians 15:28.
7. Ephesians 1:9,10.
8. St Matthew 18:23–35.

CHAPTER 10

1. See Bowden, John, *Jesus, the Unanswered Questions*, S.C.M. Press, London, 1988. Chapter 3, 'What can we really know about Jesus?', in particular addresses the problems of certain knowledge about the historical Jesus.
2. The Catholic Apostolic church took shape in 1835 with the conviction that the End was near. Twelve Apostles were chosen to be the sources of ministry in the new church, but no provision was made for passing on their powers – since the End was near. When it did not come, ministerial offices, vacated through death, could not be refilled and the last remaining congregations dispersed in the 1960s.
3. Romans 5:19: 'For as by one man's disobedience many were made sinners.'
4. I Corinthians 15:22.
5. I Corinthians 15:47.
6. I Corinthians 15:48–9.
7. Romans 6:3ff.
8. Galatians 2:20: 'I have been crucified with Christ; it is no longer I who live, but Christ who lives in me.'
9. St John 8:58.
10. St John 1:1.
11. Hebrews 13:8.
12. Revelation 22:13.
13. *The Roman Missal*, Sunday Preface no 4.
14. Ephesians 1:4.
15. St Luke 3:10–14.
16. St Luke 19:1–8.
17. Hebrews 10.
18. St Mark 4.
19. Romans 7:24.
20. II Corinthians 12:2.
21. Jung, Carl G., *Myths, Dreams, and Reflections*, Fontana, London, 1983, p. 343.
22. Schleiermacher, Friedrich, *On Religion: Speeches to its Cultured Despisers*, trans. T.N. Tice, John Knox Press, Richmond, Virginia, 1969.
23. Acts 15:28.
24. I John 4:1.

CHAPTER 11

1. Aulen, Gustav, *Christus Victor*.
2. II Corinthians 10:5.
3. St Anselm, *Cur Deus Homo*.
4. No. 273 in *The New English Hymnal*, Canterbury Press, Norwich, 1986.
5. Jung, Carl G., *Answer to Job*, Routledge and Kegan Paul, London, 1984. He writes: 'Just as man must suffer from God, so God must suffer from man. Otherwise there can be no reconciliation between the two' (p. 85).
6. Eliade, Mircea, *Patterns in Comparative Religion*, Sheed and Ward, London, 1958, p. 38ff.
7. Jung, Carl G., *Memories, Dreams, Reflections*, Fontana, London, 1983, p. 369.
8. St John 1:3.
9. St John 10:30.
10. Grillmeier, Aloys, *Christ in Christian Tradition*, trans. J. Bowden, Mowbray, London, 1965, has a very full account of the development of the doctrine of the person of Christ.
11. A quotation from the Athanasian Creed which is quoted at greater length on p. 132 above.
12. I borrow these translations of, respectively, 'hypostasis' and 'ousia' from Prestige, G.L., *God in Patristic Thought*, Heinemann, London, 1936 (reprinted SPCK, London, 1952), p. xxix. He describes the Trinitarian controversies of the patristic age and valiantly attempts to make them comprehensible and credible to the modern mind. His own final formulation is that 'in God there are three divine organs of God-consciousness, but one centre of divine self-consciousness' (p. 301).
13. Armstrong, Karen, *A History of God*, Heinemann, London, 1993. The distinction to which I refer is on p. 138.
14. Miller, David L., in *Three Faces of God*, Fortress Press, USA, connects Karpman's trios with the Trinity.
15. I quote from the Church of England's *Book of Common Prayer*, 1662.
16. *New English Hymnal*, no. 159. *Carmina Gaedelica* is the main source of Celtic prayers of this kind. There are many collections of translated extracts available.
17. Adam, David, *The Edge of Glory*, SPCK, London, 1985, p. 11.
18. Pope Leo, 'The Tome of Leo' as it is generally known is Epistle xxviii of Leo (to Flavian) and was approved as orthodox by the Council of Chalcedon in AD 451.

CHAPTER 12

1. St Matthew 10:30.
2. St Matthew 7:7.
3. St Mark 14:36.
4. Freud, in *The Interpretation of Dreams*, wrote: 'they [dreams] replace logical connection by simultaneity in time' (Standard Edition, Vol. 18, p. 28). Matters that are logically connected appear together. However, in this sense 'logical connection' does not mean 'causation', and in the same passage Freud asserts that the sequence of cause and effect is maintained in dreams. This seems anomalous, but *some* asymmetric logic is obviously present in dreams, or there would be no content to them at all!
5. Colossians 3:16.
6. Bloom, Archbishop Anthony, *Living Prayer*, Darton, Longman and Todd, London, 1966, p. 67.
7. In my view, however, the more mature faith becomes, the less is this true, and the attitude attained is of leaving the future in the hands of God, in accordance with the prayer, 'Thy will be done'.
8. From, 'O What their Joy and their Glory shall be'. *New English Hymnal*, Canterbury Press, Norwich, 1986, no. 432.
9. From 'Light's Abode, Celestial Salem', *New English Hymnal*, no. 401.
10. See p. 123 above.
11. Whitehead, Alfred North, *Process and Reality*, Macmillan, London, 1929. His distinction between a *primordial* nature of God, devoid of consciousness, and a *consequent* nature of God which is conscious (and which is coming to be) has some parallel with the thesis of this book.
12. de Chardin, Pierre Teilhard, *The Phenomenon of Man*, published in French in 1955, by Editions de Seuil; first English edition, Collins, London, 1959. He writes: 'Some sort of unanimity will reign over the entire mass of the noosphere. The final convergence will take place *in peace*' (p. 316).
13. Daniel 3:16.

CHAPTER 13

1. I acknowledge influence here from Amos Wilder, *Jesus' Parables and the War of Myths*, SPCK, London, 1982.
2. Farrer, Austin, 'An English Appreciation', in *Kerygma and Myth Vol. 1*, SPCK, London, 1953, p. 213.
3. Yeats, W.B., in *The Second Coming*.
4. Donne, John, XXVI Sermons (1660) 29 February. 1627/8.

Glossary of Key Terms

Asymmetric Logic: Common sense reasoning, often described as 'classical' or 'Aristotelian' logic.

Symmetric Logic: The way of 'reasoning' of the Unconscious. As first described by Ignacio Matte Blanco it is characterised by two principles; generalisation (p. 25ff) and symmetry (p. 29). As reformulated by the author symmetric logic has three laws:

Opposition: A proposition gives rise to its *opposite* (p. 33f)

Reflection: A proposition gives rise to a reflexive proposition in which two terms change places (p. 34 and 29)

Rotation: A proposition about three terms give rise to two further propositions as the terms change place by *rotating* (p. 36).

Bi-logic: This means simply 'double logic'. The theory that the mind uses both asymmetric and symmetric logic is the theory that it uses *bi-logic* or operates *bi-logically*.

Bi-modal: A step in 'reasoning' that conforms to the laws of both logics – for example, *'John is close to Mary'* implies by the (symmetric) law of reflection that *'Mary is close to John'*. This is also true, obviously, in asymmetric logic. The deduction that leads from the first to the second assertion is therefore a *bi-modal* one (p. 98f, 109f, 144).

The Unconscious: The word is used in its psychoanalytic sense, stemming from Freud, to refer to a deep and generally inaccessible aspect of the mind. Freud's work is mainly concerned with the **repressed contents** of the Unconscious, painful matters against admitting which into consciousness there is a resistance (p. 18). Freud acknowledged the existence of **unrepressed contents** also (p. 83–5). Jung's attention was mainly directed to these. Matte Blanco, within the Freudian tradition, explored these also. Jung believed that beneath the **personal Unconscious** lay a **collective Unconscious** (p. 84) which in some sense was common to the whole human race.

Primary and Secondary Process: In Freud the workings of Unconscious are described as **primary process**, while conscious thinking is generally **secondary process** (p. 17). Matte Blanco discovered that primary process mainly (though not exclusively) uses symmetric logic, and secondary process mainly (though not exclusively) uses asymmetric logic.

Characteristics of the Unconscious: Freud described five principal characteristics: timelessness (p. 32), condensation (p. 48), displacement (p. 48), non-contradiction (p. 50) and the equivalence of fantasy and reality (p. 54). Matte Blanco introduced *placelessness* in parallel to timelessness (p. 46). The author argues that condensation and displacement are special cases of *the equivalence of part and whole*, a characteristic arising from Matte Blanco's 'principle of generalisation' (p. 28). The five, thus revised, give rise in speech to **the modalities** (see below).

The Modalities of language: The modalities are expressions in language of the characteristics of the Unconscious (as revised by Matte Blanco and the author). They are tabulated on page 55.

The Unconscious of God: The ultimate depth of the Unconscious in which no distinctions can be made. It is argued that this relates to the goal of the mystics – the eternal, infinite, All and Nothing, beyond the distinction of being and non-being. This is aptly described as God, but perhaps as only one aspect of God – hence the analogical term, 'the Unconscious of God' (see p. 60).

The Consciousness of God: The aspect of God of which particular assertions can be made. If it claimed that God acts, or has some kind of concrete existence, then another aspect (besides 'the Unconscious of God') is under discussion. By analogy, this may be called 'the Consciousness of God' (see p. 60).

The Attributes of God: The term used here in its classical theological sense to cover eternity, infinity, omnipresence, indivisibility and so forth. For a tabulation of the comparison between the attributes of God and the characteristics of the Unconscious see page 75.

The following terms relate to figure 3.1 (page 39)
Mental processes may be more or less unconscious, and are also more or less characterised by symmetric logic. The graph plots one against the other.

The Orthobola: This is simply the line of correlation where the unconscious depth of a mental process **correlates** with the degree to which symmetric logic is implicit in it (p. 41). The theory advanced by the author is that 'sane and normal' processes lie on the orthobola: the use of symmetric logic is appropriate to the unconscious and aberrations arise where asymmetric logic is used at great unconscious depth – whereas asymmetric logic is appropriate to wholly conscious states (uninfluenced by emotion, for example) and more error results from using symmetric logic. The application to the mystical journey is found on p. 67, and to religion in general throughout chapter 13.

Scylla: Some mental processes deviate from the orthobola in that more asymmetric logic is present than the unconscious depth would normally demand. This is the region of Scylla – the rocks (p. 40). For the application of this to religion, see pages 65–67, 96, 98f, 147, 149).

Charybdis: Some processes deviate from the orthobola in that less asymmetric logic is present than the unconscious depth would normally demand. This is the region of Charybdis – the whirlpool. For the application of this to religion, see the same pages as for Scylla.

Diabola: The author advances the hypothesis that mental processes and states that lie in Scylla may transform into a corresponding point in the region of Charybdis, and *vice versa*. On the graph, such corresponding points lie on lines straddling the Orthobola which are called 'diabolas' (p. 41). There are therefore countless diabolas, but only one Orthobola. A connection with mysticism is suggested on page 67. Other religious applications are in chapter 13.

Transitional Space: The middle area of the graph intermediate between consciousness and unconsciousness, in which they may overlap. Dreams, speech charged with emotion, poetry and myth correspond to this area of the graph. In transitional space conscious matters may submerge into the unconscious, and the unconscious unfold into consciousness.

Index of Names and Significant Works

Jung, Carl Gustav 2, 3, 20, 85,
    119, 129

Klein, Melanie 17, 23

Lacan, Jacques 19
Lamech 94–95

Macquarrie, John 20, 70
Matte Blanco, Ignacio 23–4, 21,
    23–4, 26–42, 52, 62
Meyendorff, John 61
Moses 97–98

Noah 95

On Metapsychology, Freud,
    Sigmund 13
Origin of Religion, The, Freud,
    Sigmund 13

Patrick, St 132
Paul, St 106–108, 113–116, 118,
    126–127

Rahner, Karl 20, 59
Ramsey, Rt Revd Michael 16
Rayner, Eric, *Unconscious Logic* 26
Robinson, John, *Honest to God* 2, 8,
    16

Roman Catholic church 6, 116

Shakespeare, William, quoted 4,
    53, 54
Sigmund Freud, Life and Work,
    Jones, Ernest 13
Soskice, Janet, *Metaphor and
    Religious Language* 48–49
Summa Theologiae, Aquinas, St
    Thomas 10, 69
Systematic Theology, Tillich, Paul
    68–69

Thinking, Feeling and Being, Matte
    Blanco, Ignacio 23
Tillich, Paul Johannes 8, 20, 68–69
Traherne, Thomas, *Poems,
    Centuries and Three
    Thanksgivings* 9, 66, 70–71,
    101

Unconscious as Infinite Sets, The,
    Matte Blanco, Ignacio 23, 24,
    28, 29
Ussher, Archbishop James 82

White, Victor, *God and the
    Unconscious* 2, 20–21
Whitehead, Alfred North 20, 143
Wittgenstein, Ludwig 23, 78